Jacob Chastain's *Writefully Empowered* shows teachers how to bring the inner lives of our young writers into the world, moving them from compliance to engagement. It is an essential book for teachers looking to implement a workshop approach, written with warmth and passion. I highly recommend it for all secondary ELA teachers.

—**Kelly Gallagher,** author of *180 Days and 4 Essential Studies*

Jacob Chastain's excitement for unlocking students' potential as writers is palpable and contagious. Through insightful and memorable takeaways, *Writefully Empowered* is a needed guide for creating vibrant conditions and opportunities that both respect and amplify student voice so that young people can put their stamp on the world.

—**Anindya Kundu,** author of *The Power of Student Agency*

The nuts and bolts—and soul—of the writing workshop are gathered in this useful text that invites authenticity, practicality, and glorious writing.

—**Jeff Anderson,** author of the *Patterns of Power* series

A persuasive and crucial read for any writing teacher wishing to be more skillful, equitable, and joyful. In *Writefully Empowered*, Jacob Chastain illuminates what's possible for writers of all ages when authenticity, freedom, and agency become central to teaching and learning. A courageous, trailblazing book!

—**Regie Routman,** author of *Literacy Essentials: Engagement, Excellence, and Equity for All Learners*

Master teacher Jacob Chastain's book is a reminder to all teachers that writing is "deeply personal, powerful, and transformative." His call to offer students choice of topic, genre, and audience, and time to write from the heart in school enables each student to enter the writing life by exploring and developing the stories, opinions, and values that shape who they are and who they hope to become.

—**Laura Robb,** author of *Guided Practice for Reading Growth* and *Read, Talk, Write*

Compelling and timely, real and refreshing, *Writefully Empowered* is a must-read primer for anyone considering how they could revolutionize the writing workshop. Jacob offers practical strategies with an approach that gets results. Read this book to empower your students to have a love for writing.

—**Amen Rahh,** best-selling author of *Revolutionary School Culture* and principal

WRITEFULLY EMPOWERED

WRITEFULLY EMPOWERED

EMPOWERED

A **MANIFESTO** OF
POSSIBILITIES
IN THE **WRITING**
WORKSHOP

JACOB CHASTAIN

Writefully Empowered: A Manifesto of Possibilities in the Writing Workshop
© 2022 Jacob Chastain

This book is available at special discounts when purchased in quantity for educational purposes or for use as premiums, promotions, or fundraisers. For inquiries and details, contact the publisher at books@daveburgessconsulting.com.

Published by Dave Burgess Consulting, Inc.
San Diego, CA
DaveBurgessConsulting.com

Library of Congress Control Number: 2022931316
Paperback ISBN: 978-1-956306-13-2
Ebook ISBN: 978-1-956306-14-9

Cover design by Sarah Flood-Baumann
Interior design by Liz Schreiter
Edited and produced by Reading List Editorial
ReadingListEditorial.com

This book is dedicated to (in alphabetical order):

Cyanna Boone, Angelina Cardenas, Viviana Castro, Elise DeArmond, Makayla Dennis, Kamoria Ellis, Selena Espinoza, Xavier Garza, Leandro Guerrero, Yomeyra Hernandez, Adraiya Hill, Franco Lopez, Aubree Martinez, Joselyn Martinez, Micaela Martinez, KMO, Liliana Perrin, Chloe Peters, Natalie R., Jaqueline Rivas, Hailey Rosales, Addison Stevens, Cyriss Taylor, Brooklyn Tillman, and the many other students who were a part of our writing workshop but did not want to publish their work for the public.

Each of you helped shape this book in more ways than I can describe here. Your voices brought it to life. You have all been such a large part of my world and teaching career. I am forever grateful and thankful to know each of you.

Many of you have been through hell and back, yet you are here, in this book, showing what happens when honesty is put to the page. You are here, illuminating the world with your light.

Keep shining, all of you. I'll always be in your corner.

CONTENTS

A MANIFESTO OF POSSIBILITIES

The time has come to shift how we think about writing in our schools. Writing has come to be synonymous with following strict outlines, responding to prompts, and awaiting irrefutable judgment from the teacher for a final verdict on the quality of a piece. Writing has been dehumanized, for the most part, by a system that's overly obsessed with grades and with quantitative data over qualitative data. I propose we shift away from this limiting system and look at the writing our students are doing (and the writing we are doing with them) as the act of bringing our inner lives, our voices, and our souls into the world around us. Writing is far more than just responding to stimuli or performing for a grade. It is intrinsically tied to the self—our hearts, thoughts, feelings, and desires. It is deeply personal, powerful, and transformative. I propose that our classrooms should be places that honor this deeper understanding of what it means to bring our inner lives into the world, concurrently honoring the lives of everyone in the writing workshop.

There is value in talking with students about what they're writing, why they're writing, and the writing of others. There is value in students talking with teachers about writing and teachers talking with teachers about writing. Yet many of us (much like our students) haven't really spent any quality time writing for authentic purposes, which means we also haven't spent time talking about writing in authentic ways. Our writing knowledge has been primarily forged in the furnaces of college essays, whose fires were lit by our grade school grammar practice. Hardly an empowering mythology to set us on a course of discovery.

Of course, there are some educators who come into the profession as writers first. They have had a wide variety of writing experiences, both in creating and talking about the act of creating. They lead students on a path of discovery, or at least they want to, and you can see and feel this energy in their classes. If there is one rule in teaching that I find applicable to all classes and grades, it's that kids do, say, and think what their teachers model (whether the teachers are aware of it or not).

Unfortunately, freedom and purpose seem to be the exception in writing instruction, rather than the rule. Writing gets the steady diet of drills, rules, and limitations imposed by stale curriculum and less-than-inspired prompts, or focused writing activities full of colorful and whimsical fonts that are bought online in the name of fun. It's as if, as an educational community, we believe writing can't be free, student driven, or exciting because writing just isn't those things, right? Rules take precedence over practice and exploration. Colorful activities take the place of the actual excitement of creating pieces that are uniquely powerful and meaningful to the students and their audience.

Writing is seen as a bridge to interaction with content, rather than the content itself. We have students write to *respond*, *answer*, and *explain*, yet we rarely have students write for their own purposes. Rarely, we have them write for the sake of writing and all the benefits that come with it. If we do let them write, driven by their own purposes and desires, we designate this time to Freewriting Friday or Write What You Want Wednesdays. This is the equivalent of saying, "Your voice matters, but could you please just use it for a minimal amount of time during the week?" We say, subconsciously, "There's real learning to be had, after all, and you won't learn how to write or think by writing or thinking whatever you like!"

At the risk of getting political, there is a reason why governments who want more power choose to silence their opponents. The most tyrannical leaders opt for book burnings rather than real political discourse. They silence the authors and the poets. The human voice is the most powerful tool in the world. It can overthrow governments, reveal the reality of myths, and unveil the secrets of the universe.

It might sound dramatic to talk about student choice and freedom in their writing in this way, but this is precisely why we must shift to this larger view of what it is we are doing when we rightfully empower students to use their voices. When we let—no, push—for students to use their voices for their own purposes, we give back to them what is rightfully theirs as human beings: the tools to shape the world in their own image.

Let me be perfectly clear here: when we rightfully empower students to use their voices in writing, we are not giving them something they do not have already; we are removing restricting systems that have stolen, silenced, and manipulated student voice into a preapproved box of thoughts, structures, and purposes.

In traditional terms, empowerment is something the powerful give to the powerless. A rightfully empowered student is a student who is free to use their voice because it is theirs to use. It's their power already. A rightfully empowered classroom honors this and operates within this shifted paradigm. Teachers are not the saviors in the rightfully empowered classroom. Students do not need saving. They need us, and the systems we build and work within, to get out of the way and support them for who they are on their individual journeys through understanding, processing, and meaning making.

I told my story in my memoir, *Teach Me, Teacher*. In that book, I described how I felt schools and the teachers within them saved me from a family consumed by drugs and violence. While I stand by the feeling that I was saved by my teachers and schools, in truth, I was saved because the educators in my life allowed me to be me. I showed up every day with trauma heavy on my heart and mind, and so many of my teachers gave me a place to release my anxiety, hate, and fear in healthy ways. They were not saviors, but their actions saved me. They were educators who served me in the ways that I needed, despite the systems around them. My perspective on my life and what education has meant for me has evolved over the years. If any contradictions exist between the insights addressed in that book and this one, it is due to this personal growth and not due to a lack of grounding in my own beliefs. I see now I was rightfully empowered to have agency over my experiences, how I processed them, and the questions I pursued as I created meaning out of my own pain.

In contrast, when we limit student voice, when we insist that students can't learn to write by writing with guidance from a knowledgeable and passionate teacher, or within their own interests or choices, we tell them their voices don't matter. We might add *yet* to the end of that sentence, implying they must write to conventions before meaning, but the damage is already done. Their only hope for achieving the real power of their voices after years of indoctrination into this reductionist take on writing education is to find it themselves. Not impossible, but a scary game to be playing with our students' lives.

This book has been designed to be consumed quickly in hopes that it can catalyze teachers to take on and embrace a rightfully empowered writing workshop. To keep this book short, I have opted to not address the reading side of the workshop equation. However, it should be noted and taken to heart that a great writing workshop is supported and indeed driven by the reading choices students make. Independent reading is just as important as independent writing. Students should have access to a variety of books from authors they connect with and to stories that resonate with their lived experiences and the experiences of

4

those outside of their immediate communities and cultures. Enriched reading lives create enriched writing.

This book isn't a how-to, though elements of that exist, and it isn't meant to be prescriptive, though I offer some guidance on specific pedagogical moves teachers can make. I have tried to balance actionable tasks teachers can take today with the belief that what works in my class, or with a specific class, might not be what works in someone else's. While there are nonnegotiables in a rightfully empowered writing workshop, such as plenty of time to write daily in class, there are just as many options to substitute to fit your unique needs. I am not selling or offering a program. I am inviting you into a dynamic shift in perspective on how we approach writing with our students.

I support the pedagogy and teaching philosophy I advocate for with student work from my own sixth- and seventh-grade workshop in the form of microprose, musings, rants, and lots of poetry. You will note a lack of essays—the primary form of writing present in many curricula and classrooms. This is primarily because essays are almost always assigned, and none of the pieces shared from my students' writing portfolios were assigned by me. Students chose to make each piece of their own volition, guided by the power and structure of the writing workshop. I believe the best demonstration of the effectiveness of the guidance offered in this book is to show you many examples, across a variety of students, of the work they chose to do given freedom, time, and a safe place to use their voices.

It does no one any good to talk about rightfully empowered students without showing exactly what rightfully empowered students sound like. Too often, we talk about kids, not with them. Too often, we tell students what to write, when what we need to do is listen to what they are already trying to say.

What to Expect

At the very center of this book is a call for a writing workshop that has freedom, equity, and equality of opportunity at the core of every choice. As used in this book, *freedom* is choice in writing topic, purpose, and form. *Equity* is ensuring each writer receives unique and personalized support in their writing progress, with a focus on goals and growth. *Equality of opportunity* is the act of setting up a workshop that removes traditional barriers, empowering students to interact with, and work to master, the act of writing in ways that honor where they are and who they can come to be. Focusing on freedom, equity, and equality of opportunity allows us to support our students' voices, provide the tools to sharpen the precision of their writing, and rightfully empower their passions and purposes to take on the challenges of today and tomorrow. All three of these concepts together create a rightfully empowered writing workshop.

Opportunity is created when we repudiate the idea that our voices should fit into a standardized box. The human spirit is not standardized. Being empowered to use and hone their voices in the classroom should be a fundamental right for all students in their wonderful diversities, including, but not limited to, their neuro, racial, and gender diversities. This is not to be confused or conflated with a call for equality of outcome, or the idea that everyone ends up in the exact same place. While an empowered writing workshop aims to have every student improve their command of language in writing, striving for equality of outcome runs the risk of not honoring the diversity present in all our classrooms because people with vast differences will have vastly different outcomes. Besides, the only way to achieve true equality of outcome is to control, and control is a barrier to crafting an empowered writing workshop. Striving for equality of opportunity, freedom, and an equitable framework aligns us more with honoring diversity because it supports the notion that people are different, and thus require different approaches, amounts of time, and kinds of support to get to where they need to be. When this is our focus in the workshop, startling growth in student ability becomes the norm, and student empowerment transitions from ideal to reality.

While you might not need this book on writing to learn how to teach writers, it's possible that you need this book to learn how to teach yourself how to be and think like a writer. It's possible that you need it to break away from your own indoctrination into the so-called ways of school writing. It's possible that you need it to be pushed into loosening control over your students so that they can forge their own paths through thinking, speaking, and writing. It's possible that you need it to rightfully empower your own voice so you can turn around and rightfully empower your students' voices—and be the catalyst for change among your colleagues. It's possible that you need a manifesto of possibilities to realize that students will write if we let them and that, oftentimes, the biggest impediment to student growth and empowerment . . . is us. And that is where we will begin.

Chapters 1–7 follow the creation and facilitation of a rightfully empowered writing workshop. We begin with what writers need, classroom setup, and routines and move on to how the mini-lesson, independent work time, and conferring with students all work together to create the energy of the workshop over time.

Chapters 8–11 deal with satellite issues—questions that teachers often contend with, such as how to track growth, where to get grades from and how to assess, how to advocate for equitable practices in a school or on a team where equity isn't a primary concern, and how to handle when students write about trauma, pain, and the darker parts of their lived experiences.

The final chapter summarizes why I believe we should be creating rightfully empowered writing workshops in all schools. It also highlights several pieces from the students I have been lucky enough to learn with over the last two years. They deserve the last word in a book that is not only about them but for them.

CHAPTER ONE
WHAT WRITERS NEED

This book is largely concerned with writers and what they need. It is about the real and powerful human beings in our care and how to offer guidance as they discover self-empowerment. We are not here to learn how to decipher curriculum or prepare for some test. As prevalent, pervasive, and pernicious as both may well be, writers really don't give a damn. And why should they? Writing is the empowerment of a voice. It is the act of taking something internal (thought) and manifesting it physically, using a variety of agreed-upon symbols and marks designed to clarify meaning. Why on earth would writers who are truly and rightfully empowered to use their voices care at all about the whims of mandates and dictations designed to control and coerce a mind into obedience?

They don't, and as their writing teacher and fellow writer, you shouldn't, either—at least, not in a manner that hurts your effectiveness in the world of the writing workshop.

Writers Need Room to Grow

Like plants, writers need room to grow. They need space. When writers are too close together, say, in a stock writing assignment where everyone is writing about the same thing at the same pace, they begin to compete for resources. They fight to put their roots down. In this lack of space, they get intertwined and grow far less than they would if they were given more room. Their minds become diseased by a lack of nutrients, and they grow weak. Their yield is small. Their writer lives are short, sporadic, and need to be replanted often because of an inability to reproduce results with so little nutrition to fuel their growth.

A singular focus on prewritten curriculum with no attachment to the students sitting in your classroom or on baneful standardized test taking only yields poorly spaced-out writers and poorly equipped teachers to water them. We aren't interested in creating writers who do what they are told to do. We are interested in our writing workshops being a field with enough land, rain, and sunlight to fuel every writer's growth. We are interested in giving them enough space, time, resources, and energy to blossom in the ways they are uniquely designed for, not the ways that people who will never see them have designed for them. This growth comes to light as we see their writing take on keener focus and deeper purpose, and when they have greater control over their word choice and pieces.

If we approach the teaching of writing with anything but the writer in mind, we have already failed them.

Writers Need to Be Seen as Writers

Of course, this assumes we are thinking of the students in our classes as writers at all. In many cases, we aren't. We see lethargic students approach the page with about as much enthusiasm as we approach tedious household chores. We see them take an entire class to write a sentence, and that sentence probably isn't even very "good." We watch as they struggle to write to the prompts we assign or stick to a singular topic and expand upon it within a one-page essay.

We see students as *not writers* first and wonder how we make them writers, when in fact, students are already writers when they walk into our classrooms. They might not all be essayists, novelists, playwrights, poets, memoirists, songwriters, or even technical writers, but that's such a narrow view of what a writer is. Some might be bloggers or avid tweeters. Some might be Facebook status creators or Instagram post makers. Many are content creators. Some might be the Stephen King of text messages.

Even outside of these forms of writing, we write in our heads. We create stories out of our lives, situations, and dreams and ideas. We craft intricate plot lines for ourselves where we are simultaneously the hero and the villain. We argue with ourselves and have constant battles of will with our own vices and habits. We pray. We send mental letters to the heavens and curse our demons with intense prose that would set the paper ablaze with its fury if we bothered to jot it down. If writing is thinking on paper, and it is, then our thoughts are a form of writing. Call it prewriting if you like, but don't misinterpret a lack of hand movement on paper as not writing.

It's vastly important for us to broaden our thinking about what constitutes writing, because it frees us from constraints that hold us and our students back. We have been conditioned to think of writing as something that's only done within physical space, ignoring all the thought and emotional processing that comes before the act of turning thought into words on a page. When we ignore this process, our teaching practices become more about *seeing* students write than about supporting everything that goes into quality writing itself. Every decision we make about writing becomes about seeing: we want to see the outline, multiple drafts, revisions, color-coded peer edits, etc. This puts an overemphasis on production before purpose and volume before volition.

When we approach the classroom with the mind-set that writing is just the few academic genres school curriculum leans toward, and that writing is a binary process that happens only when we can see it happening, then we will train thousands, if not millions, of students to believe that their words are unworthy of being written unless they bend them to fit inside very specific boxes.

What's the point of an education if it doesn't open up one's life, mind, and soul to possibility? Hell, what's the point of an English classroom that doesn't give this possibility wings?

Writers Need to Be Free

Year after year, young people are told they have to stay within a certain box in writing—oftentimes quite literally, as we force students to fill in outlines for standard essay structures. Worse, we tell them they can't even start to write when they have an idea. They must write about writing, using one of a million versions of an outline, and then they must get approval from us to move forward. This is usually followed by a day of drafting "hooks" to begin their papers (again, approved by the teacher), and only after all of this prework can they possibly start drafting whatever it is they are working on. The topic is chosen by the teacher, or if the students are lucky, they have a range of topics to choose from (the illusion of choice). They move in lockstep all the way through the writing process until they hit the due date in unison. Maybe there is a day of revision and peer editing built in to this process to pay tribute to collaboration, but that's not guaranteed. Once they turn it in, they wait for the red-penned paper—or comment-riddled Google Doc—to come back to them with a grade on it. Then they forget they ever wrote the piece at all, often wishing they hadn't because of the empty feedback received in the form of corrections.

For many students, they will only write in class when there is an assignment and only practice writing in the forms of grammar correction and worksheets. Not because they want to, but because this is the only time they are given the opportunity to write. These days, schools substitute worksheets with digital programs sold to school districts as solutions for students' gap in mastery of writing mechanics, but the essential idea is the same.

We want students to learn how to write well, but we spend far more time looking at writing in parts and pieces rather than writing as a whole. They rarely get to put it together in authentic ways. Students need to be educated on the building blocks of the written word, but not at the expense of self-expression and the act of writing full pieces they choose to write. If we want lessons on craft, grammar, and form to stick with our students, it's imperative that we give them the time to use the skills taught to create for their own purposes.

Unfortunately, students will rarely get to choose what they want to write about, and if it's a year when there is a writing state test, students being encouraged to write in any genre outside of what would be tested on is often completely out of the question.

As a new teacher, this is how I taught writing. I would set up assignments for students to tackle, maybe provide a rubric for them to use, and then sit back as the papers came in. Sure, I would step in and point out an error in a student's writing as they worked, but I didn't really talk to them about their writing, just what they needed to improve. I focused more on mechanics than ideas and more on writing than the writer.

Later I thought I was being progressive in my grammar instruction by opting to move away from writing worksheets and instead using a Google Slide with two to three sentences in need of correction. I thought I was in the know of how to make writing engaging because I created cool and flashy writing *activities* that got students moving and talking.

Looking back at these early years, I know students had fun in my class. They enjoyed the energy of the lessons and how I brought my personal flavor to each activity. Even when we teach less effectively, we can still rely on our personalities to carry a lot of the weight of engagement—and I certainly did. Unfortunately, this leads us to believe that we are being effective, when in reality, we are just being entertaining.

I know now that I wasn't helping form writers in any meaningful scale. I might have moved a few writers into a positive relationship with writing, but given the importance of writing to the lives of my students, effecting change for a few just isn't good enough.

I was teaching school and its curriculum, and I was teaching to the test. I wasn't teaching the writers in front of me, and I wasn't talking with them about their writing or really reading much of it. Why would I, when they are all writing about the same thing? After three papers on the same subject, I could pretty much tell you what the next middle schooler would say in their piece.

Without deep and meaningful instruction on what makes an effective topic and how meaning dictates form, as well as the freedom to choose topics and styles of writing, underpracticed writers can only do so much. Writers with little experience forming words, creating unique ideas from stale concepts, or pushing the boundaries around them to make room for original takes on a subject don't write pieces worth reading (or writing, if we're being honest).

The teachers who are looking out at, or thinking about, their students as they read this book and wondering why they won't write must stop and ask themselves what they are doing to diminish the students' desire to write. What systems, protocols, and classroom structures are sucking the resources away from their roots? If we are only offering lifeless assignments drudged up from the pile of assignments we have always used, or worse, were designed by another teacher with other students and goals in mind, then we will never get writers who are filled with life and energy to use their voices.

Serving the writers in our classrooms requires us to get rid of everything possible that doesn't strive to do just that. We must cut the excess, the fluff, and the stuff of school and get down to the real work of writing.

Writers Need to Create

There is a tangible energy in a room when writers are left alone to create. When students are focused on pieces they care about, when they are empowered by their own purposes and are driven to bring their voices to the page, the classroom hums with excitement and joy. When students eagerly open their writing journals to begin a new draft or revisit a work in progress, not out of compliance, but because they genuinely care about their work, you can't imagine a class any other way. Once you experience the power of student agency in a workshop that's supported by a knowledgeable workshop leader, there is no turning back. It becomes a belief that this is what the writing classroom, or what writing time, should be. When the human spirit is free to be what it needs to be today, in this moment, truth is revealed, and truth beckons us to join it.

Writing is gritty, edgy, and ferocious. It's kind, therapeutic, and loving. It's sad, lonely, and lost. Writing, especially writing from young people, is so in your face with its raw power and *I don't give a damn about your feelings, this is what I think* attitude, that to treat it with anything but the utmost respect and genuine care is to limit the fire of what it means to be youthful. This is the time for them to grow by doing, to learn by creating, and to begin the process of becoming. Self-realization and introspection are not tools for just the lucky few who have the time and wherewithal to receive them. These tools belong to all our students by right, by purpose, and hopefully by design, as we reimagine our classrooms and writing workshops for the better.

CHAPTER TWO
WORKSHOP DESIGN, ROUTINE, AND STRUCTURE

Every student has a bias toward the subjects they like, for one reason or another. Some love math because they think well with numbers, or love social studies because they had a teacher one year who dressed up as historical figures. Some love English because they have a positive relationship with books, or art because they draw and doodle at every opportunity. We can't control whether our students like the subject we teach. In some cases, a student might already hate your room simply because you teach English, and English sucks, so there! That's why we need to design workshops that our students actually want to be in—physical spaces as well as routines and structures that foster positive associations. If we walk into a room or place that we greatly enjoy and understand how the space functions for our needs, then our emotions and thinking will be more positive. If this feeling is strong enough, it will even let our bad day melt away, allowing us to check our problems at the door. We will be more open to ideas, changes, and even challenges in this environment. Happiness breeds curiosity, and a curious writer is a good writer.

On the other hand, if we enter a place we loathe, have associated with failure, or are unsure how it functions for our needs, then our emotions and thoughts will be filled to the brim with negativity. Our walls will come up, and we will isolate ourselves in a world of annoyance, and even hate, if the emotion is strong enough. And since misery loves company, all of our current problems, perceived problems, and future problems come flooding in to drown us.

Regardless of whether students love or hate what you teach, you can win them over by designing your workshop in a way that brings not only comfort, routine, and structure, but also security and a constant demonstration that the students are who matter most.

A Classroom They Want to Be In

A mind distracted by problems, concerns, or uncertainty is a mind that will struggle to get into a creative flow of words. Students are smothered in these issues. As they move from class to class, with endless variables either hurting their day or helping, they can't help but feel overwhelmed mentally by it all. The torrent of assignments, directives, rules, procedures, notes, text messages, sounds, interruptions, tests, failures, successes, and punishments are enough to make anyone lose creativity, so it becomes the job of workshop teachers to make sure their classes mitigate these issues as much as possible.

I had the realization one year that my students went from class to class staring at white walls under fluorescent lights. As a creative person, I couldn't imagine anything worse. There is a reason people choose to write at coffee shops, after all.

I decided I wanted my class to feel like a portal to someplace other than school. I wanted the bright lights *out there* to be drowned out by the warm tones *in here*. I wanted school to be left in the hall and a feeling that students, once they cross over the threshold of my door, have entered workshop—a place of possibility.

To do this, I painted my walls a darker color, put up soft lightning, added a rug and bean bag chairs to my library, and crafted a few seating areas around the room. While I have never had a fully flexible seating arrangement, students loved being able to sit anywhere once we began our writing time. During lessons they either sat on the soft rug in front of the white board or pulled up a chair, and then for their independent practice and work time, they sat at tables or in one of the comfort areas.

My room wasn't what people would call beautiful. It wasn't filled with the most high-dollar furniture, but it was different enough that I could feel student anxiety fade when they entered. With some paint and some secondhand furniture, I provided a place that invited students in. This didn't break the bank or take me months to decorate. All it took was a brief examination of my room and the willingness to make each corner offer something a little different for kids to experience.

I have repeated this process many times, even taking an old busted portable and completely beautifying it with a coat of paint, rugs, and lights. It has worked every single time. Students may not come out and say how much they love your room and what you have done with it, but you will know they enjoy it as you see their stress begin to dissolve in your room. That is the magic we are looking for.

Obviously, many teachers might have restrictions on what they can do with their rooms. In such a case, here are two suggestions to get around them.

One, ask your admin for creative ideas on how to stay within the rules and still spice up your space. Partnering with leaders on campus is always a great idea. Teachers often forget the power of presenting a well-thought-out idea to leaders in hopes of collaboration rather than simple approval. Most leaders are more willing to collaborate than to give a blanket yes or no.

Two, ask for forgiveness later. Sometimes you have to push the boundaries just a bit.

Regardless of the path you choose for creating a space worthy of a lively writing workshop, it's important that you have clearly defined areas. Areas to consider, among others, are:

- **A writing space** where students can sprawl out, get in the zone, and craft their words into meaningful pieces. This can be a specific area or all around the room—whatever your space allows for. Providing freedom in where they write is a surprisingly simple way to get students excited about this time. If they look forward to moving to a specific spot in the room, then they are already coming to the page with an energy that supports the act of writing deeply and meaningfully.

- **A publishing area** where students can type up their work, if technology is available, or create final drafts and add them to their writing portfolios. Having students publish regularly will keep them working toward a goal.

- **An area where you hold their writing portfolios.** I prefer, and my students have preferred, physical writing portfolios because it makes the publishing process more concrete, but this can be digitized in a Google Drive folder or another digital format if you have the means or desire to do so.

- **A wall of published work on display** that gets added to regularly. Use the end of the grading period as the time to pick pieces that will make the wall. Set criteria for how pieces are chosen, such as pieces that represent the unit best. These guidelines will help ensure that students do not get discouraged when a piece does not make it on the wall. Instead, they will actively try to create pieces inspired by your mini-lessons, thus keeping curriculum in line with freedom of choice. Students will come to expect it and will love seeing what makes it up on the wall. Students often read these pieces as inspiration for their own work too. What we put on the walls of our classrooms shows students what we really care about and value.

- **A classroom library** where kids can explore books and read. Great books are models for great writing. They are the best teachers for how to write well. Consider organizing the library using the same categories as your school library to support access in and outside of your classroom. It will teach them to navigate the bigger space more easily and help them understand the difference between genres. Assign each genre a color, label each book with a piece of colored tape, and print out a chart for reference. The colored tape will help keep the library organized and help students find the genre they're looking for. It will also show you what is being read the most and what you need to buy more of.

While the five areas listed are not exhaustive, I believe they are the most practical and essential for your class design to reflect the work you want to happen every day. There are other options, if you have the space or need. For example, some workshop-focused educators have also suggested that there be areas where students can confer with one another. I suggest starting with what is listed above, and as your workshop develops, decide if you should add other areas or modify to suit the needs of your workshop. Designing a welcoming, well-organized physical environment creates the foundation for the workshop that will take place within it.

Routine and Structure

Students need structure. They need to know what to expect. Without this, they automatically have more anxiety about your space, which makes your goals, and theirs, harder to reach.

For the uninitiated, the workshop structure can be summed up as: mini-lesson, goal setting, student work time supported by a teacher conferring with individuals or groups, and a debrief. While this format can be played with and altered to fit your needs and style, I can't say enough about the power of following this format, at least in the beginning of your workshop journey.

It might sound boring to have the same thing happen every day, but the only thing that stays the same is the structure. Just because you begin every day with a mini-lesson does not mean it has to be just like the one from yesterday. On the contrary, research confirms that students are more likely to explore when offered novelty, and the best way to achieve novelty in the writing workshop is to have mini-lessons that surprise them, inspire them, and shock them out of the daily habit of school. As you develop as a workshop teacher, you may add in activities such as read alouds or extended writing time, or you might mix up the formula to suit the needs of your students. The beauty of workshop is its flexibility, but flexibility can also dilute the focus of the workshop. Like most things in teaching, it is a balancing act you have to watch and manage as time goes on.

A predictable structure is the key to a workshop that becomes self-operating. Predictable structure is conducive to what writers need. Haruki Murakami, the famous and best-selling author of *1Q84* puts it nicely. Talking about his schedule when writing a book he says, "The repetition itself becomes the important thing." Hemingway famously said that he wrote every morning after the sun came up. Steven Pressfield, author of *The War of Art*, speaks about the power of his rituals and the effects they have on his writing and creative life. In a writing workshop, routine is not simply classroom management, it is a ritual to free the mind to work.

Security

The power of writing lies in its ability to hold truth with words on the page. If writers are not being honest in their writing, the writing they are doing is for someone else. While it's obvious that writers, at times, need to write for others, writers need to bleed on the page for themselves long before they ever try to offer truth for others to consume.

We often ask young writers to write for others in class—as early as the very first day. We create *get to know each other* activities where students write about themselves, their lives, and their experiences, all with sharing as the goal. But writers need *get to know yourself* activities before we have them write so that others can know about them.

If we push writers into sharing their work too soon, they begin to build walls around their minds. They learn early on that writing is a place to hide, not expose. They learn that writing is designed for others to judge, not for them to examine the world they live in. They learn that if they say the right thing, rather than the true thing, they will be praised for it.

The social pressures alone are enough to make young writers bend to the norm around them, which makes these early writing tasks that permeate grades useless, if our goal is to create empowered writers. You cannot be empowered if you are intimately involved in writing what others want. Writers must be allowed to embrace their right to be honest on the page. They must believe wholeheartedly that they have this freedom and be taught to use it in a trusting, safe, and secure environment. The writing workshop can be such a place.

We must diligently present this to the writers in our classrooms. From day one, we must show students that they are safe to explore unpopular ideas, different routes of thought, and beliefs that defy categorization, as well as to reflect on experiences that often do not fit neatly in the square rooms of the school. We must move beyond lip service and demonstrate security in small ways that build up over time.

Begin by showing students that their writing is theirs. It doesn't belong to anyone else until they allow it to be. This might seem scary for teachers still entrenched in the tradition of "I assign, you do," but it is essential to not skip this step. If students are told they have freedom but always know that what they write will be read and judged without their consent, they will never be empowered enough to burn down injustice with their lines or heal their souls with an honest and raw form of forgiveness.

Some teachers have opted to show students this by offering them the option of folding the piece of paper over if they do not want it to be read. I believe this is a great way to show students that they own their writing, but an easier and more trusting approach is to simply ask to read a student's writing and respect the answer if it is a no. Tell them early on that this will be the case. Tell them that when you come by for a writing conference you will talk with them, but before a word is read, you will always ask for permission and respect their decision either way. Not everything needs to be read, I tell them. As the writer, you get to decide what you keep for yourself and what you offer to others.

This is a sacred contract. Once it is made, it is done under the most ancient and divine laws of the human spirit. If you break it, it will take weeks or possibly months to build that trust again with your student. In truth, that trust may never return. There is an art and strategy to the writing conference that can help drive this trust and get writers to open up to you, the teacher, but this topic warrants its own chapter and will be addressed there.

The only time when this contract between the workshop leader (you) and the writer should be breached is if you have any concern that the writer is a danger to themselves or others. It is your moral obligation to report such matters, in accordance with your district's policies, to protect the writers in your care. Students must feel secure, and that means we protect them when they cannot protect themselves.

The other major aspect of security in the writing workshop is showing students that we are here to explore interesting, new, and at times (as our grade level permits) daring ideas. Modeling this in our mini-lessons is the most direct and constant way to show students that we are here to explore. There will be no punishment for thinking outside of the box. The texts we bring into the class should inspire new thinking, not solidify the same truisms that flood classrooms everywhere.

For example, rather than repeating the same old clichés about the importance of being a good friend, let's examine pieces that look through the eyes of someone who has been betrayed, analyzing how that betrayal manifests in word choice, structure, and meaning.

Rather than talking about being honest, let's read a piece that is honest about hard topics. Don't hide from realities such as gender identity, race, drug abuse, or even depression and suicide. If you are teaching in secondary classrooms, it might be hard to accept, but your students are more aware of these issues than you want to believe. Hiding from these issues and pretending that they do not affect the lives of middle and high schoolers is delusional at best, and destructive at worst. Teachers often want to skirt these issues and opt for happier pieces and stories with so-called good moral messages. Just because students know about these bigger problems doesn't mean we should push them into the classroom, some say. This might be followed or supported by the claim that it isn't a teacher's job to address issues like racial discrimination or abuse.

To that, I offer two thoughts:

One, if we want students to write honestly about their lives, we must honor the lives they live. We must show them that even their harshest experiences, which are the ones they need to address in writing, are free to be discussed here in this safe place. We should be able to talk about the darkest and most confusing corners of the human experience and not be shamed for addressing the truth.

Two, as educators, shouldn't we take an active role in helping students think, address, and process the harder aspects of their existence? We don't have to be counselors or therapists, but we have to give them the proper tools to think about the disturbing, painful, and confusing realities they encounter. Adults spend so much time hiding from the real experiences kids go through that students begin to feel shame in their pain and thus find alternative ways to cope. We talk about wanting to put kids on a positive path away from drug abuse and behaviors that could quite literally ruin their lives, but we never offer the tools or freedom to address what causes those behaviors in the first place.

What's the point of an education if it only addresses academics? Serving the whole child, the whole young adult, is about giving them the tools to navigate the real world. One of the biggest criticisms of the education system is that it does not prepare students for the real world, and it is a valid one, at times. As writing workshop teachers, we can change this fact. We can be the difference.

In the end, what we are designing is a classroom which tells students that they are what matters most. We are putting their work on the walls. We are crafting lessons that are real and relevant to their lives. We are letting them own their writing and control when they release it for others to read. We are honoring their thoughts, ideas, beliefs, experiences, and emotions by allowing them to exist, without judgment, within the classroom. We are talking with them as if they are writers, not as if they are performing animals dancing for another treat.

Writing workshop is a place of real work. We aren't concerned with the fluff of school. Writing workshop teachers should be focused on a singular purpose—the writers in their rooms, and the truths they have to tell.

A Final Note on Workshop Design

Each teacher reading this will have different limitations based on school or district directives. Designing a workshop that serves all writers is less about what you can't do and more about what you can do. It would be exhausting and probably impossible to address every possible issue you may have with following the guidance in this chapter and to offer alternatives, but I can say that your class is what you make it. You can be defeated by limitations imposed on you, or you can use them to your advantage.

You can also choose which hills to die on. Stressing about due dates, school supplies, and other minor issues distracts from the hard work of writing and thinking about writing.

Writing should be due when it is finished. Give students the freedom to decide when a piece is done and ready for publication in the class. If desired, you can add a soft deadline of having one piece (or more) published per grading period. Even so, this should be more of a goal, rather than a mandate, much like it is in real life. Sure, emails must be replied to in a timely manner and deadlines are imposed by jobs and contracts, but writing in schools should be about joy and love first—how else will they ever get enough practice to be successful at meeting those deadlines imposed on them later in life? If students do not meet your requirement of pieces to be published, investigate why. Look at their work and see if it is enough to get the grade. Were they writing every day? Why weren't they able to make it through a piece? Odds are, if you are meeting with students constantly in writing workshop, you have a grasp on how much work they are doing and can put in an accurate grade, even if they didn't publish. More importantly, if you are meeting with students constantly, you will be able to understand what held them up from getting to the publishing phase and support them in meaningful ways that lead them there.

Freedom requires goals, but freedom is not beholden to goals. Keep working with students until they do publish, and then start it all again. Once students get one piece done, and are honored in this process, they will begin to increase their productivity and publish more.

Finally, when it comes to supplies such as pencils, journals, paper, etc., it's a waste of time to punish students for not having such things. Give them a pencil if they need one and some paper if they forget their journals at home. It really isn't that big of a deal. Be an advocate for your students and ask if the school can fund a collection of supplies to give kids as needed. Odds are the money is there. Use it and be done with it.

Writing is too important to waste energy on making kids feel bad about not having a pencil to write with. For the love of God, how often do we show up to meetings without something to write with? Move on and get over it. There is work to do.

CHAPTER THREE
THE INVITATION TO WRITE

Prompts that tell students what to write are where great quotes go to die. The internet and workbooks have made sure of it. Doing a simple search for prompts geared toward middle or high school writers yields thousands of lists with quotes to respond to and think about. Even worse, it yields hackneyed observations or ideas that encourage writers to explain why it's good to have friends or to write about the biggest surprise in their life. Themes like these are not bad by themselves, but taken out of context and without a powerful anchor or model text, they are atrocious sources of inspiration.

Writing is the single most rigorous, demanding, freeing, and expressive form of art that can occur in a standard classroom. When we reduce this process to simple responses and bland prompts, we literally strip the writer of creative power. Classrooms that use a prompt for every piece of writing are classrooms that cater to students who can play the game of school writing, ignoring how inequitable this game is. We see the same five students churn out relatively decent essays about their role models and places they'd

THE INVITATION TO WRITE

like to visit, and the same five students respond to quotes from Albert Einstein and Michael Jordan in standard five-paragraph essays. All the while, we are left wondering why the writing being done is boring to read and why the other writers in the room are so stalled.

Prompting has become synonymous with writing instruction. We approach writers with sound-bite sentences and expect them to be able to fill pages with beautiful words, only to be disappointed that they can barely craft a paragraph. How many would-be-great writing teachers decide they hate teaching writing because all they have ever read in student writing are responses to prompts that they found the night before the assignment was given? Worse, how many would-be-great writers decide they hate writing because all they were ever asked to do was respond to ideas created by anonymous people on the internet?

Prompts are training wheels for a hover car. The minds of children and young adults soar with ideas, thoughts, emotions, observations, questions, rants, and reflections. They might not be the thoughts traditional school models want, but they are there, and they can be quite striking in their power. Young people are bursting to tell everyone what they think about the world and the events happening around them. They are clawing to share what pissed them off in the hallway yesterday and reflect on whether they should stay with their current boyfriend or girlfriend. They want to talk about what it is like to not be able to trust any adult in their lives, or what the loss of a grandfather makes them think about.

Welo
Selena Espinoza

I really wish I got to see you before COVID. . .before the heart attack. I still have so many things to say to you. I just want one more hug. One more "I'll see you next year, Ma!" One more night at your house. One more time trying to teach us how to fish. One more time talking about how we should move in with you. One more time riding the lawn mower and the little cars

around the neighborhood. One more time feeding the cats,
even though you said not to.

Beyond writing from pure personal experience, as Selena did in her
piece "Welo," powerful models, excerpts, and full novels and poems
may prompt students to think and create. Often though, we take these
sources of inspiration and control how students respond to them.
There is certainly value in analyzing great literature and writing pieces
in response to it, but we should question how much emphasis is put on
this type of writing and the control we add to it. On the surface, what
may seem to be a rigorous activity involving literature analysis may
actually be students playing the game of school to get a grade. When
students are writing to please the teacher in a specific and almost sub-
servient way, rigor is lowered drastically.

The mind has been wired by millions of years of evolution to be
curious and to seek abstract answers. It's what drove us to mold things
from stone and why we took our hands and painted images of animals
deep inside ancient caves. The mind doesn't need prompts to wonder
what the meaning of life is, or to question the value of a friendship
gone sour, or to feel something from a great piece of literature and
analyze it; it needs freedom. It needs room to wander and explore.

Kids Will Write if We Get Out of the Way

Unfortunately, many teachers suppress this need, sometimes con-
sciously but mostly accidentally, by weighing down writers with
training wheels teachers think they need. By the time writers get to
your class, especially if you are a secondary teacher, many have become
wary of freedom. They have been trained to resist it. Year after year of
"Don't write that, write this" has a certain effect on the creative process.

You can spot these writers quickly. They constantly stare at blank
pages. They say they don't have anything to write about. They wait
patiently for teachers to supply them with prompts or topic ideas—
almost Pavlovian, in a way.

Whether I am speaking on a podcast or at a teacher workshop I am facilitating, I am usually approached by educators exasperated because their kids just won't write. They try to inspire them and to offer plenty of time, but the results are the same. Then, feeling rushed by the need to make it through the curriculum, they say writing time slowly fades away. The struggle is real and valid. Don't feel alone if this is you.

The good news is that there is a surprisingly simple method to break the heavy training wheels off and let the student mind soar again. It is a process of bringing students into reading and thinking like writers. It is a focus on language, purpose, meaning, and structure.

Whether the training wheels were put on students by you or the years of teachers before you is irrelevant, because all that writers need to return to their natural state of curiosity is a simple invitation to do so.

The Power of an Invitation

A person is much happier to accept an invitation than a command. An invitation is an inclusive gesture. It says, "Hey, I have something I want you to be a part of. There's a great place I want to show you." A command says, "It doesn't matter if you like it or hate it, you're coming with me." One makes someone a part of something special by choice and one demands compliance.

If writing is about the voice of the person doing the writing—and it is—then commanding a writer to write is a contradiction at best, and a betrayal at worst. The rightfully empowered writer is not beckoned with the threat of a bad grade or some other form of punishment. Rather, they are invited out to show themselves, to run free in the sunlight, and to change the world as they see fit.

Of course, if it were as easy as that books very much about inviting writers, such as Jeff Anderson's fantastic *Patterns of Power* series or Kelly Gallagher and Penny Kittle's *180 Days* wouldn't be needed, and writers in every classroom would be creating great art and standing up for what they believe in.

The invitation teachers give to writers is a delicate process. It hinges on many aspects of a lesson, a school, a classroom, and the students within that space. As educators, we must take in the variables around us and use them to our advantage. We must know our students and their backgrounds and offer pieces that model, reflect, provide insight, and commune with their lives. These do not have to be long novel studies, and they definitely do not need to be the same books that have been used in classrooms since our parents and grandparents were students. While those works can be valuable, short, targeted, and powerful excerpts of longer pieces or poems are enough to teach with and inspire great writing. Moreover, studying short pieces allows for a depth of study in a shorter amount of time, which allows writers to move on quickly to the work they need to do individually. If students connect to an excerpt from a longer work, then they can pursue it more. If they don't, rather than suffering through an entire unit and disengaging, they can move on when the next text is used.

The invitation is not to take a piece and tie it to "a chair with rope and torture a confession out of it," as Billy Collins so eloquently puts it. The invitation to explore a piece, the act of asking writers, What do you notice? and then wandering together through meaning-making and thought-adventuring is a sensational experience. For some reason, many educators have come to an agreed-upon narrative that students can't notice something wonderful about words unless we tell them why those words are wonderful. Of course, as with most groupthink and with a moment of thought, this is demonstrably wrong. Young or inexperienced writers might not have academic language to express why a metaphor fits the mood and theme of a poem, but they can point out that they were affected by it. They can share how a line made them feel. They can see structure and comment on what it does for the piece visually. The worst thing we can do to art is make it accessible only through staunch academia. Art was here before academia, and it will be here after.

The Music of Writing

Music creation and writing prose and poetry are a part of the same family. They are identical in many ways, yet we approach each far differently. If you were to walk into a music classroom and ask the students, Who likes music in here? every kid would raise a hand. If you did the same in an average English classroom and asked, Who likes reading or writing? you'd get a mixed bag—and probably a lot fewer hands than the teacher would hope. Yet in those same English classes, teachers often start by defining what a simile is ad nauseam, examining sentence fragments, and detailing rules of complex and compound sentences, rather than start with building or cultivating a love for the written word.

On the other hand, music majors and musicians alike decide to learn the technical and academic aspects of music because they love it first. They connect to it so much that they want to know the ins and outs of it. They didn't start with being commanded to write out notations in odd time signatures or to analyze long pieces of music coupled with a pile of worksheets to help think about the piece. They loved music first and chose to learn more.

Of course, if we want to be honest, many musicians don't ever learn how to explain the songs they write in any musical form whatsoever. Yet, they still create songs that change the world. Jimi Hendrix famously didn't read or write music and neither did the Beatles. Does this diminish their creations?

Though we allow musicians that freedom, we still expect students who don't even like reading or writing to care about the more technical aspects of crafting a piece. Does it even *really* matter if students can name parts of a sentence as much as some teachers and curriculum writers think it does?

Regardless of your answer to the above question, the fact remains that many of our students have never been given the opportunity to love words. Whether it's fiction, nonfiction, or poetry, students haven't been given the invitation to simply say what they liked, or didn't like, about what was written. Many simply haven't been exposed to enough writing to even know what they like and don't like. While this book is singularly focused on writers and the writing workshop, it should be noted that students need to be reading voraciously to write well. Handing students three to five books a year to read at a collective pace isn't enough to create readers and writers with perspective on their own taste. It isn't enough to get them to discover genuinely amazing prose and poetry that not only connects with their own experiences but also gives them insight into how to navigate them.

Each teacher is limited by time in different ways. Every single one of us is forced to make sacrifices in order to accomplish what we must in the classroom. However, we cannot sacrifice reading time any more than we can sacrifice writing time. They fuel and drive one another in directions other activities cannot. Because many students live in what experts call *book deserts*, we must be vigilant in surrounding students with great literature, poetry, letters, memoirs, articles, and words that they choose to read independently, as well as within the lessons we bring.

Unlike books, music is pervasive in most modern lives; it plays everywhere. Students hear it at school, on YouTube, social media, and on streaming services. The barrier to entry is also lower. It takes less effort to listen to a song than it does to read a piece (which is why read alouds are powerful, regardless of the age you are teaching). The written word, outside of texting and social media, isn't as pervasive, and this creates a problem to overcome in the classroom.

Offer Texts That Reflect Our Students' World

The workshop teacher becomes a constant investigator into powerful excerpts and pieces that will provide students with not only tools to learn from but also words to live by and engage with. Knowing who your writers are as people is key to making this work long-term. Talking with them to learn what they think and what drives them as people will guide you to model texts that will fire them up. Just using what is provided to you through your district's curriculum or the textbook will be a lesson in frustration, and most likely, a lesson in a severely nondiverse reading life in style, not to mention race, gender, and religion. The steady and voluminous diet that we feed students in the workshop should reflect the real world—their world. For too long it hasn't, and it's clear that the world today, at least here in the United States, is evidence enough that this needs to change. Mandated curriculum or not, our students need to be exposed to great texts that verify their own existence and offer insight into others' experiences. The invitation these texts offer is the platform that empowered writers stand on.

High school teachers are often more comfortable than middle school teachers using texts that might be seen as controversial, which is a nice way of saying texts that are deemed unfit for the classroom because of misguided or misinformed censorship. Because of the age group being served in high schools, teachers are able to bring in varied, interesting, and relevant texts that are powerful invitations to students.

Middle school teachers, however, face a different world. They operate within the transition years from childhood to adolescence and young adulthood, which are rife with complicated developments. Oftentimes it can feel like half the students have barely begun to question what adults have told them, and the other half are already in complete rebellion to what they've been told. All the while, parents are doing their best to guide their children and to make sure that they are getting the best education from their teachers—staying active and vigilant to what is being talked about in class. Middle school teachers, in an attempt to navigate such complicated waters, accidentally end up coddling parents and trying to regulate students, crafting lessons around lukewarm pieces in the process.

In my years as a middle school teacher, teaching grades six through eight, there is a fact I've learned that I imagine is inescapable for someone teaching this age group: middle schoolers are ready to talk about the complicated world and its problems. Watering down subjects in middle school is as sinful as ignoring their problems altogether.

The world middle schoolers are beginning to realize exists is hitting them left and right, figuratively, literally, and politically. Illusions are falling away and their faith and trust in what they have always believed is beginning to waver. Their innocence is beginning to evolve into an adolescent maturity. For some, it has already fallen away entirely. To ignore subjects like racism, gender identity, equality, equity, police brutality, faith in religion (and lack thereof), abuse, drug addiction, and the feelings of love and loss is to ignore what they are already grappling with. Rightfully empowering writers isn't just offering them supportive phrases and gestures of freedom, it's about breaking the illusion that school happens here, and life happens there. School is about understanding life. School is about giving young minds the tools and varied perspectives they can use in their real world to navigate its tribulations more effectively. It's about showing them the keys to the kingdom so that they can open the door, realize there is no kingdom, and begin to build their own home in this vast and untamed landscape of reality. And if not a home, then a path toward a place of understanding through a direct facing of their own reality.

The words of Micaela and Viviana, seventh graders, echo this sentiment eloquently:

Change
Micaela Martinez

Everything I used to love
now bores me.

I'm over it,
and I hate myself
for it.

I used to sleep
to wake up,

now I sleep to
escape everyone.

How did this happen?

How did it all change?

Outlet
Viviana Castro

I'm sorry that my way of dealing
with my pain is writing about it.
It may seem like I'm just looking for
attention, but it's for my own good.
I guess, it's like if I don't let it out,
it will be locked up inside me and
hurt me more than it already does.
It's better for my words to hurt the pages than me.
I'm sorry that I don't write all sunshine
and rainbows. I'm sorry I'm not the
happy and perfect girl you want me to be.
I'm not gonna start writing about love
or about the happiest day of my life.
I'm not gonna write about flowers and sunsets.
I'm gonna write about the voices in my head

and the darkness within me.

I'm gonna write about the world as I see it.

I'm going to burn away the shadows with the light of my truth.

As you give students more ways to connect to the world around them, you will see your students increasingly accept the invitation to explore and write. At first, it will feel like a trap. Freedom usually does to kids, because it usually is. But what we are talking about here, together, is a real freedom. A freedom to explore life and all that is in it. As teachers, we show pieces that examine a part of life and then invite students to do the same.

If the pieces used to invite students into this process are powerful and targeted to your writers, then you will see them transform into poets, essayists, and creatives. You will see elements of your mini-lessons being used in their writing. You'll know a piece is powerful, and your mini-lesson effective, when you make your rounds with writers and see lines, words, phrases, structures, patterns, and ideas echoed in their varied creations. Remember those pieces, because they may work again next year, but also remember that the kids you get next year will be different and might need something else to inspire them.

Making Connections

When I showed my students the spoken-word poem "Hair" by the wonderful author of *The Poet X*, Elizabeth Acevedo, students were inspired in so many different ways. We watched Acevedo speak in her impassioned style, read her words, and analyzed our favorite lines and talked about how we related to the ideas in the piece. I invited them to share their own experiences that connected with what Acevedo said in the poem, and then we wrote.

My Hair

Kamoria Ellis

My hair is like the wind gushing in your soul, as wavy and beautiful as the waves pouring down on the sand, like my hair down my shoulders. So beautiful and graceful, yet a tsunami.

My hair shows the brown skin, gold in the sun. Sparkles like when the sun catches a glimpse of my eyes.

My hair doesn't match any others.
No green eyes, no skin from the winter snow.

It's the brown of the early fall, when the sun shines like a regular sunny day, tricking you when you feel the temperature of a cold breeze of the wind saying "good morning." The brown from deserts going for miles, never ends. The brown from me.

All brown.
All my brown.
My hair.

Seems as though all the colors are in me, but does not have to show it for you to know.

My hair gets off-guard when a family member says "talofa" to you, but is still figuring out how to reply back.

My brown silky curls levitate up and down, like a feather so light that it gets confused if it's going up or down, so it goes both, still ending up on the ground.

My hair is so gentle, but it's the definition of chaotic. Just like our dances, graceful and beautiful, but has so much meaning into each move it makes.

It makes my middle-aged aunties scream
"CCCCCCCHHHHHOOOOOOO," makes me proud of myself,

knowing your elders liked the dance you brought them.
Earning the scream that says "I'm proud" is one of the best for my hair.

Represents my culture, my color, my life, my hair.

Every Black, Tongan, Samoan string in my hair, is what brings me to life.

It's my hair, the hair that fits me. Nobody else's.

Likewise, I shared the poem called "Accents" by Denice Frohman and got an equal response from many writers. My students laughed and nodded along with the poem and how it's presented, and then we discussed connections with it. I invited them to identify a line that resonated with them and asked them to explain why in their journals. We talked about the use and play of language, and then I invited them to use all of these elements and their connections in their own writing.

Too What?   Yomeyra Hernandez

Am I too much,
or too little?
Am I too weird?
Too crazy ?
Too funny?
Too joyful?
Too annoying?
Too happy?
Too much energy?
Is it too much Spanish,
or not enough English?
Pues cómo quieres que hable?
Me oíste!?
I apologize for not speaking clearly enough for you.

When you see elements or ideas from a mini-lesson and model texts show up in student writing, you know you had a win with that lesson. When they don't, you missed the mark.

At the beginning of a school year, or even after a break, this is common. Lessons won't land with the impact you wanted. But as you confer with students, read their writing, and begin to know them as human beings, you will be able to bring pieces and lessons to them that beckon their participation as students and as writers.

Once students know that they are always invited and included, and they feel that in the very fabric of how you run your writing workshop, students will act with the assumption that the invitation is always on the table. This is when your workshop begins to soar above the standard English class.

CHAPTER FOUR
THE MINI-LESSON AS A CATALYST

Young and inexperienced writers make a lot of mistakes—mistakes in grammar and word usage, structural decisions, and various other craft errors that cause a clouding of meaning in a piece (the true danger of mistakes in writing, I'd argue). Some young writers make more mistakes than others, and many seasoned writers make mistakes as well. It's a part of the process and should be understood as essential, not just something to fix. English teachers, myself included, tend to push toward always fixing. In reality, we should broaden our approach to not only getting students to what they feel driven to write, but also to write it well.

In education, you can never be sure of the students you are getting in a given year, or what their writing background is. If you have a campus culture unified around writing, and you are getting students mostly from inside the school, then this process becomes easier. But for the grades that serve as entry points into a school, the skill of incoming writers can be massively varied. This can lead to teachers looking at all of the writers' problems at once and feeling overwhelmed or even defeated.

This is understandable. With the pressures of testing and the curriculum weighing on educators, it's easy to feel at a loss about how to get writers writing well—or even writing better than yesterday. In an act of overcorrection, teachers will often seize control of the writing class, forcing students into lockstep movements through the writing process and making generalized scaffolds for whatever task students are being asked to do.

At first, this might look like it yields the results desired. Kids make slow-but-steady progress on their drafts and can answer basic questions about hooks, introductions, and body paragraphs. But on further examination, the drafts are stilted and deeply resemble each other. Unified, lockstep writing-instruction creates papers that get turned in at the rhythm of marching soldiers. Passion in the pieces is vague—if present at all—and the formula used to create these pieces is so predictable that reading them can become a chore.

And despite the fact that this lockstep approach is meant to improve student writing, many pieces are still riddled with errors that muddy the purpose the writer has for them. This leaves the teacher back at square one. So how can we teach our students to write in the way that will best let their intended meaning shine through?

When writers write, they wander with the curiosity of early humans exploring a newly discovered land. Especially when they're just starting out, less-experienced writers take odd detours and find themselves lost with very little to help guide themselves out of a dense forest of disconnected ideas and sentences. When we see this happening in a workshop, it's tempting to immediately grab control, demand that students start with pre-planning, then move on to opening sentences, intros, and the like—but this takes power away from them. It removes discovery. It removes rigor.

Instead, teachers must show these young explorers how to find their way before they go, and teach them short, actionable tasks for how to find their way out of confusion and aimlessness. A skillful guide can teach someone how to look for trails that will lead to water and keep the explorer on track. Some trails are easier than others—and the more adventurous the writer's ambitions, ideas, or emotions are the harder it will be to find trails that have been walked before, but it can be done. All writers can be taught how to find what works and what doesn't. Understanding and internalizing the mini-lesson as a catalyst to action is the key to being an effective guide for the writers in your classroom.

Short and Sweet Lessons

Writing workshop teachers are guides. They do not demand that explorers take specific paths, though specific paths can be shown to those who need them. They do not speak as the final authority, but as companions who have walked the paths themselves and who want to help others on their journeys.

To do this, the teacher facilitates a short mini-lesson. Fifteen to twenty minutes is a fantastic goal. Any shorter of a lesson and they run the risk of being too brisk and losing the writers in front of them. Any longer, they risk disengagement and boredom in the students.

The focus of the lesson should be on just one concept, or at most a few targeted concepts, being worked on within the curriculum or the standards for that day. The suggested length of the mini-lesson implies a focused approach to what is taught or examined during this time, but I want to be clear: the workshop teacher should avoid, as much as possible, loading mini-lessons with a bunch of new material to learn. If the concepts or material being learned is new, the teacher should address less in the mini-lesson. If they are retreading ground, they will be able to add more into this time.

Keeping lessons short and focused on an idea, structure, pattern, or style is key to getting writers to accept the invitation to analyze, borrow, and imitate in their own work. The more complex a lesson becomes or the more flash used in the name of engagement, the more transfer of knowledge will diminish from the lesson to their independent work. Students are most engaged when they understand what is being taught. They don't need to be assigned elaborate pieces in most cases—although these can be effective for other purposes. They need focused and clear instruction on the craft choices made by writers of varied backgrounds and purposes.

Furthermore, knowing your students on a deep and human level will increase the odds that your mini-lessons become something special to the writers in the space. They will become engaged if the texts being explored in the workshop are relevant to their lives and applicable to their own work.

Be mindful of what is really driving the focus of the mini-lesson. Is it your interest or theirs? Is it relevant to you, or was it inspired by real talk with students in your class the day or week before? The best ideas for your mini-lessons will come from talking with your students about their problems, interests, and wonderings, then finding texts that connect to those aspects of their lives. (Conferring with your students is the best and most natural way to get to know students in the workshop, and we will address that more in chapter 5.)

The number of mini-lessons that can be taught is endless when they are focused on what's relevant to the lives of the writers in the workshop. There are as many mini-lessons as there are ideas to be thought about or explored. These lessons are intimately designed to connect to the students. It isn't so much about the topic being discussed as it is about the students' connection to the topic.

For example: if your lesson involves an article examining an injustice in the world, the connection might be how students have personally felt about or dealt with injustice in their lives. Because the writers are young, they might not have written about such complex topics and feelings before. As the guide, you should help them understand and process these feelings by carefully selecting texts that you know your students will relate to and work with them to understand how other writers were able to create effective pieces on the subject. Asking questions like "What craft moves did they make?" "How did they frame their perspective within the text structure?" and "Why were we moved by the piece?" are all great ways to encourage not only the enjoyment of a piece, but also the bridge-building between the content studied and the work to be done. Teaching students the process of actively consuming texts and synthesizing texts with their lives, their world, and their beliefs is deep and needed work in the classroom. This means being open to a unit evolving based on discussions that happen during mini-lessons and conferences. It's hard to stick to a lesson plan in a workshop that honors and empowers student voice, because their voice is what we are aiming to support.

It's in lessons that foreground big ideas, exploring them in a variety of ways relatable to young minds, that we begin showing the more technical aspects of writing. We grab students' attention by offering mirrors and windows into and out of their own lives, and then we show them how to use language to achieve their own goals as they interact with their connections to the many pieces, books, and excerpts we bring into our lessons. The mini-lesson catalyzes action in their own writing lives.

As stated in the introduction, this book is not a strict how-to. However, sometimes understanding the flow of a mini-lesson or conceptualizing what one actually looks like can be challenging. The following sections serve as a guide for how to begin mini-lessons in your own workshop journey. It is not the only way to construct a mini-lesson and it is not a strict protocol. It is simply a mini-lesson in context.

A Mini-Lesson in Context

Begin by handing students a copy of the featured text that they can write on. Choose whether to have students read the passage silently to themselves or to have it read out loud by a strong reader or the teacher. Reading the initial pass out loud is a great way to scaffold a difficult text, and also a strong choice to bring a piece to life in the early morning or post-lunch lull of a classroom. You can also read aloud on the second pass. Experiment to see which way works best. What works might change depending on the week, day, or lesson.

On the first pass, have students jot down their initial ideas and reactions to the piece in silence. If this is the first or second time they have done this style of response, it might take a moment for them to be able to write something. If they are really stuck, or the piece you chose isn't connecting as well as you would have hoped, consider silently writing and projecting your own response, giving students a model for their thinking. Many will borrow from what you're writing if they are stuck, and others will simply see you writing and begin jotting down their own ideas in response.

Of course, you can *always* project your own response. You don't need to wait for them to be stuck, but it's also valuable to stay mobile while students are jotting down their ideas. It shows them, subconsciously, that you are engaged with them even when they are working alone. Attempt to balance your movement around the room with being tied down to your own writing space. Both show solidarity in different ways.

Write, Share, Listen, and Speak

Once students have written their responses, let them discuss their responses in a Turn and Talk or Think and Share. As they speak, move from pair to pair listening in, offering a point at times or posing questions to spur further discussion. Consider taking this conversation to the class level and allowing them to share their processed thoughts for the class to hear. This is a great way to formatively assess where your students are in their thinking, both individually and as a class.

By moving around the room and formatively assessing students as they share in a low-stakes activity, you will be equipped to highlight the great points students are making, as well as to elevate the thinking of students who might be struggling. By letting them write, discuss, and share you are creating an easy-to-learn habit that will slowly engrain itself into how your writers process text. This will make them stronger metacognitive readers and writers.

After knowing how students responded to the piece and where their heads are at with it, and more importantly, whether they are engaged with it, take another pass through the piece. If the first pass was read aloud, consider having students read it again on their own. If the first pass was read silently, consider reading it aloud. Front load this second read-through with a focus on a key question or two to help students dive deeper into the piece, now that they are familiar with it. Basing these questions off the lesson standards for the day is a best practice, but your purpose and focus for the day will naturally alter the types of questions you lead with.

After the second pass through the piece, repeat the process of students thinking and sharing from pass one, but with an emphasis on the questions you used to set up the second read-through. Once you have reached the whole-class discussion phase for the second time, enliven this discussion with additional questions to support a deep dive into the piece as you hear where students are in their thinking.

These questions should be guides and opportunities for spontaneous inspiration. Early on, preplanning these questions will be key, but as you gain experience, you will be able to work off the energy and focus of students naturally, making every lesson and read-through a wonderful experience of discovery with your students, rather than something you drag them through. There is something special about questions, observations, and musings generated by the teacher and the students during a mini-lesson.

Again, depending on your goals for the day, your questions might be more focused on reading or writing. In general, a powerful frame used to plan for levels of questioning is to begin by reading a piece as a reader, then flipping to reading it as a writer. Experience a piece how the author intended, then analyze it as a student of the craft. Repeating this process with your students will build the skills necessary for your writers to be not only conscious consumers of great literature, but also dedicated disciples of writing.

From Experience to How

Assuming the first two passes were more reader-focused, move into the final stage of the mini-lesson and ask, How did the writer do that? What do we notice about the structure? Did the author use longer sentences to draw out a scene or emotion, or did they use short and stilted sentences to make the reader speed through a moment of anger or anxiety? Did the poem have long lines filled with description or short lines that drove the reader's eyes further down to the end of the poem? How were commas used? Em dashes? Was there punctuation at all, and why might they have capitalized certain words?

Of course, you wouldn't ask all of these questions or notice all of these aspects of a piece at once. Later in the year, when students can recall previous lessons, you might get away with addressing several in a lesson, but early-on one key aspect of a piece will do. For example, if you want to tighten up writer usage of compound and complex sentences, don't sit there and define what they are, or worse, correct wrong ones. Pick pieces or excerpts that show students compound and complex sentences, and ask what they do to support the ideas presented in the piece. Guide them to notice not what these sentences are, but how they can be effective in presenting a writer's message within a piece.

Modeling and Practice

To facilitate the transfer of knowledge from the mini-lesson to student writing itself, close out the lesson with a brief practice. Having students model a paragraph of their own after one they've read or write sentences that model the structure and shape of an interesting line in an excerpt or poem are great ways to check for understanding. If you make this a regular practice, some of the best igniters to student pieces will happen at this final step in a mini-lesson. Students will experiment in a low-stakes environment and stumble upon their own ideas and connections that drive their writing for the day. Modeling beautiful writing has a way of creating beautiful writing, and this becomes like magic to students. You will see their eyes light up as they mimic great lines and passages. That light in their eyes becomes the drive to continue writing, exploring, and engaging as thoughtful students of the craft.

Practice of this sort is also particularly useful for teaching grammar and mechanics. Once writers experience and see why a particular grammatical convention is useful for their purpose, they will begin experimenting with it. In this way, grammar becomes less about rules and guidelines and more about a tool they can use to fit their needs.

Practice helps students understand that the whole reason grammar rules exist in the first place is to serve clarity and understanding. Grammar supports meaning. Or in the words of rapper Crooked I, "The English language got to do whatever my verse say." As writers begin to home in on the ideas they want to explore, or the words they want to say, they will begin to work with new ways of writing their message. They will be more willing to use commas correctly as they see examples that they want to emulate and borrow from. The more pieces we show students, the more examples they have to borrow from and have the possibility of connecting with.

For example, I love the em dash. It's such a fun piece of grammatical expression. As examples, I showed students some prose excerpts from books in our classroom library.

When addressing these excerpts, we started with ideas first. We read and discussed them and wrote down our thoughts. As the discussion went on, I asked students what they noticed about the text and how it was put together. A group of students noticed the em dash, though they didn't call it that. Excited because I wanted to hit on this, we circled the dash and briefly jotted down its name and what it looks like it's doing in the piece. We decided as a class that it symbolizes a pause, or a sudden stop, in the writing. I then invited students to use one or both of the sentences in question as a model in their own writing.

Don't Force It

Note that in the above example, I didn't ask students to write ten sentences like what we were analyzing or write down the strictest definition of the em dash. We observed how the em dash was used in wonderful excerpts, we defined its use in our own words (briefly), and then I sent out the invitation. The simplicity of this approach is how a greater transfer of knowledge occurs. It's also how we ensure that we are fostering an equitable approach to the work of writing and understanding its many nuances. Students come to terms with what we are teaching at their own pace and as they find authentic need to do so. Belaboring a point will only yield disengagement and disinterest, while a quick mention and an invitation to use the grammatical element—not a mandate—will keep student choice at the forefront. Students that use it immediately will do so because they choose to, and students that do not may use it later, especially as you bring it up in later lessons or during conferences. They will also notice it more as they read and come across it naturally. With multiple ways for students to apply what is being learned, you can now all but guarantee that if a student does not begin to apply their learning, there is something else going on. Students who do not begin using what has been taught can be focused on in conferences or tutorials.

Stepping back in this way can be anxiety-inducing for educators used to the "I assign, you do," mentality, but it's freeing. Requiring students to always use what is talked about immediately afterward is a needless chain on creativity. Just because they do not use it today, doesn't mean they won't. Eventually, as you review earlier lessons, students will find a use for the em dash, the semicolon, or a complex sentence. And if they don't find a use for it themselves, it's because they do not see the value in it yet. Trust the process. Trust your ability to make grammar useful, and trust that your students will acclimate to the rules of writing as they develop over time.

Focusing on ideas first, and then slowly bringing writers into how they might use those ideas, is key to putting student voice first. Empower the writer, not the grammar. Remember: We are not here to teach writers to be like everyone else, never straying from the path. We are here to teach writers to focus on what they want to say, and then work on how to say it as effectively as possible. Even teachers who love grammar, who live and die by its rules, should embrace this method because students will actually use what you teach them. Student engagement, volume of work, and sense of purpose will increase as the workshop becomes a place of freedom and exploration.

CHAPTER FIVE
THE WRITING CONFERENCE AS CONNECTION

The writing conference is the heart of the writing workshop. It is the rhythm of a writing class, keeping everything alive and moving. It is the single best relationship builder, assessor, and conduit for teaching, reteaching, and intervention in a workshop environment. It is an act against the traditional models of teaching, in hopes of forging a new path with every single mind in your class. It is the act of meeting students where they are and handing them the fire that will light their way on any course they set out on.

Traditionally, teachers would stand in front of a docile class and provide information and mandates like disinterested gods, doling out punishment as needed to make sure students stayed within the proper boundaries. The writing conference dares to snub the gods of old and offer something to students quite terrifying to teachers who would want a more controlled student body: humanity.

Few actions show students that you care more than pulling up a chair and sitting with them. Doing so demonstrates to them that you are truly here to listen and offer support for their voice by meeting with them one-on-one, day in and day out.

As a teacher, I feel a thrill at the beginning of each conference session with a young writer. Conferences are the antithesis of the lockstep approach to teaching. Because you are removing barriers to students exploring their voices and allowing them to be driven by their own lives—rather than the lives school would love to push on them—no two conferences will be exactly the same. Every piece needs something different. Every writer needs something different. Teaching with equal opportunity, freedom, and equity in mind takes all of this into account.

In some ways, writing-conference sessions are the most demanding and rigorous activity you will put yourself through. By the end of a flurry of conferences in a class, you may feel mentally and physically drained. However, your teacher and creative spirit will be alive and glowing, absolutely. There isn't anything quite like a day spent exploring words, purposes, and the lives of young people. Once you get your first rush of elation from this process, you'll wonder how you ever helped students write in any other way.

There is no step-by-step approach to conferring that can be said to work every time. Due to the variation inherent in working with writers one-on-one, how could there be? Your conferences will be as varied as your students and their purposes for writing their pieces. While there are programs, packets, and beautiful graphic-organizers available to purchase online that promise to streamline conferences, there is no way those could ever come close to the effort you put into knowing each one of your students deeply, with the goal of serving each in the ways that they need to be successful in the workshop.

It's best to begin conferences with a perspective on why to confer as well as a few examples and experiential advice to guide your own work. As you become more experienced, you will develop your own way of doing conferences. You will recognize a great conference when you see or have one, as well as those that didn't work as planned.

Despite the lack of an overall system, there are a few nuts and bolts of a writing conference that are relatively standard among the practitioners who utilize this pedagogical method. These should help you get started on your own conference journey.

Duration

Writing conferences are short and sweet, much like the mini-lesson. In my own practice, I have found that most conferences last between two and five minutes. This gives me enough time to briefly check in with the writer, see where they are in their writing, and provide the guidance needed.

Some conferences can be shorter than this, serving as more of a quick check-in with a writer who is working hard on a piece. Some can also be longer than five minutes. At times, a writer may need you to dive deep into a piece to work through a particular theme or idea or work through some deep line-work in a poem. Embrace this time, but use it sparingly. Again, there isn't a hard and fast rule, but if every conference is lasting longer than five minutes, you are probably talking too much and should shift to listening more, asking a few questions, and giving the writer just enough to keep moving in their work. When the writer gets moving, you should move along.

To Schedule or Not to Schedule

Some teachers opt for having students schedule their own conferences, based on the idea that this gives students more ownership over the conference. This is well meaning, and can work, but I prefer to work through the room at my own discretion. Once writing begins I'll ask, "Who needs to see me first?" and the first three hands raised are the first three writers I go and meet with. After that, I allow the flow of needs to guide me to the next student.

Sometimes I take a systematic approach, moving from table to table in a clear order. Sometimes I skip around, meeting with students back and forth across the room. I let them raise their hands and request a conference during this time, but I reserve the right to get to them when I need to if I know that there is a writer or group of writers stuck or becoming off task.

Some writers will become dependent on you and try to confer with you as much as humanly possible. They do this because they are either stuck or lack confidence in their own ability. Another reason that I reserve the right to get to them when I can is to nudge students who lack confidence to begin trusting themselves more. If I know they have the tools and the ability to work without me and are becoming dependent on my work with them, I will pull away slightly to help them realize that they are capable already. And no, this isn't done in secret. I tell them that I'm pulling away a bit, leaving them with the expectation that they realize their skills are already present in them.

A Constant Presence

An active teacher who is constantly conferring with writers is a teacher with a well-managed workshop. If students know that you can come over to them at any point, they are more likely to self-manage their behavior when you are talking with another student. And if they don't manage well and get off task, as young people will do, it won't be for long. Workshop teachers are not at their desks grading papers, working on lesson plans, or answering emails about who wants to bring what to the potluck next week. They are too busy doing the real work of teaching, and this creates a lively and focused atmosphere that isn't easily broken by an off-task behavior here or there.

If you walk into a writing workshop during writing time, you should see the teacher doing one of two things: conferring with students at their desks or writing along with the students, possibly projecting their work as a model. Anything else is a distraction during student writing time, and should be seen as such. To put it plainly, if the teacher in the room does not honor the writing time by directly interacting and supporting writers constantly through their work, or doesn't ever do the work themselves, students will quickly realize that this is just another school task and disengage.

The moment students see workshop as just more school work—as the equivalent of doing practice math problems or a grammar worksheet—your workshop is dead. That's a hell of a grave to dig out of (though not impossible) and should be avoided at all costs by staying active throughout the time. Cut out distractions. Grading can wait. And who really wants to read email, anyway?

Engagement and Authenticity

Getting students engaged in the conference begins with you. The conference is the time for you to build and deepen relationships with your writers and to show them there isn't a *gotcha* waiting to be sprung—the conference really is designed to work for them and for their piece. Many students won't believe this, of course, because throughout their lives school and their teachers have taught them that every action is a potential gotcha. You have to put in the work and live by your word to show them why you are conferring. Even if they haven't written, a conference is not code for a scolding. It is always a meeting of a teacher and student—or more importantly—a writer and a writer and a discussion about what needs to happen next to keep the writing moving forward.

Of course, noncompliance with the expectations of the workshop does happen from time to time, but it shouldn't be your primary worry. Empower students to tackle ideas and topics meaningful to them and outright refusal to work will be an extreme rarity. More than likely, a student not writing is a symptom of a different issue and is better approached with a detective's eye rather than a superior's wrath.

Asking yourself, "What does this writer need to move forward," rather than asking, "What's my next step in punishment," will lead to better answers for a student who isn't producing work.

Getting Stuck and Unstuck

When I encounter a student in conference who is stuck or isn't producing a steady volume of work, I make sure to remind them that we are writers in this room. And you know what? Empowered writers are not slaves to timers or artificial productivity measures. They do not necessarily write consistently for thirty minutes. They pause. They think. They are not workhorses that can be pushed to keep pulling the cart. They are explorers of their own minds and souls, and exploring at such a level takes time. It takes pause. It takes a moment, or two, or even a few days to think and process through.

I tell my students that I do not expect a lot of writing, or even that they write words every single day. I tell them that if I check in on them and they didn't make visible progress on a draft, then I want them to be able to talk to me about their thinking. I let them know that I will come to them first thing tomorrow, so I want them thinking at home about what they would like to accomplish in the coming writing session. If they do not write the next day, I will take time for a longer conference to work through their work with them.

With my mind open and my desire to see words written on the page checked at the door, I approach this conference with a focus on helping the writer through whatever block they have. Maybe they need help choosing a topic or approaching their idea in a certain way. Maybe they need help starting. Whatever it is, my hope and goal for this conference is to leave them with an ability to work once I am gone. If this still does not yield results, and they come back for a third day of nothing, I will take a more direct approach and actively craft an idea with them, even writing beside them to work through starting a piece.

In most cases, a stuck writer will have something to work on after this process. Very few can last through this gradual increase in scaffolding and not have a piece they want to work on. Some do, however, and they become a constant focus for the writing teacher. Again, resist the urge to hand out zeros or punishments. If a consequence is the only tool we have in our toolbox to help stuck writers, we need to have a better toolbox.

Throughout the process, it's important to talk honestly about what writers do. If you do not know, read interviews and listen to talks from writers, or better yet, become one yourself and watch your own actions when writing. What do you do naturally? If you pause for a long time, or get stuck and don't add another word to a piece that day, are you being noncompliant? Do you deserve a zero if you didn't write a single word that day, but thought deeply about your work?

That's not to say that getting unstuck is easy. One of my students who has a tendency to flounder at the beginning of every new draft wrote the following piece after an extended period of not writing at all in class. She was frustrated with me for seemingly not helping her (though I met with her every day to discuss her writing and ideas) and frustrated with herself for not being able to write something. Eventually, she struck a vein of inspiration from a mini-lesson, when she was inspired by a line from "Space-Time Continuum," a spoken-word poem by Oompa. She went on to write the following poem:

When the Sun Shines   Addison Stevens

There will
be a day when
the sun is
shining.
Even
if you can' t
reach

it,
right now,
or
anymore.
In a day,
a
week,
or
even
a
year,
there will
be a
day
when the sun
is shining.

If I had forced this young writer to write the week before this lesson, I would have taken the power away from her and made writing more about doing school work than getting inspired and working out a piece that captured that inspiration.

Another writer, who was stuck for even longer, finally wrote this short poem after months of very little output. This piece came about after extensive conferences about their interests. Eventually, the student settled on their love for taking photos.

The Shot   Franco Lopez

Zoom in
Adjust the focus
I try to find the angle

It just can't capture her beauty
I start to get frustrated

The camera gets focused
Everything looks perfect

The picture comes out
It's what it needs to be
I show it to her
She looks happy

Zoom out
Pack up
Leave

Data Isn't Just Numbers

Being new to the process of working with students who are gradually finding words, ideas, and a sense of purpose in their writing can be stressful. At times, you may feel like nothing is getting done. The weight of curriculum guides, looming tests, and grading periods will want to force your hand and take control of the writing process. The best tool to help keep these anxieties at bay is a constant use of note-taking. Whether you use a journal, an iPad, an app on your phone, or your laptop, take notes on every writing conference. As these notes accumulate, a tapestry will start to form about every student. Taking notes like this will help ensure that you serve writers equitably. You will gravitate to certain students naturally, whether they are your strongest writers or most off-task writers, and you will need a system to make sure you reach every student, every week. Reviewing notes and seeing that you haven't conferred with a student in a few days keeps your practice honest and keeps you accountable to the quiet student's needs just as much as the eager student who would confer with you every second if they could.

Your notes will also be a great resource when your administrators ask about data. You will be able to show them data you have gathered on the writers you are working with, their work, and how they have grown over time. If you use a digital device (I like to use my iPad, Apple Pencil, and the app Notability), you can even take pictures of student writing and store them in your notes. Every student in my workshop has notes and pictures of works in progress. I take pictures of a round of revision we did together or of a first draft compared to their final draft. When I have data meetings with my administrators, I bring all of this with me and show direct evidence of growth and progress in the writing workshop.

While many sneer at the thought of using anecdotal notes as valuable data, it is a great way to judge student progress and growth, if done correctly. In writing there are few absolutes that can be judged in any standardized way. It is the effort to standardize the grading and judgment of writing that has led to the death of passionate writing in students, and one we want to avoid if we truly want to rightfully empower our students.

Quality writing is subjective, and there are ways to evaluate it based on the values of the writer and purpose for the piece. These notes play into that evaluation eventually, so keep them neat and organized for quick reference as you go deeper into the writing workshop practice. We'll look more closely at data and assessment in chapter 9.

Trust the Process

Above all else, for a writing conference to work and to continue working, you must trust the writing process. Trust that when students are empowered with freedom and equal opportunity, they will do good and honest work. Trust in your ability to be the difference for the kids in your care by setting up a workshop environment with equity in mind. You will believe this more as your practice develops and you see the results yourself.

The world we live in does not want to empower the voices of people, let alone young people. It is quite literally designed to keep those who stand outside of the norm down and controlled. By freeing students to work through their pieces, not only on their own but with you—a guide, mentor, and fellow writer, you are giving them the very things that they need to use their voice for change. The writing conference is Promethean in every aspect, and by being a diligent practitioner of it, you will hand humanity back to those who have long suffered for the lack of it.

CHAPTER SIX

AN EXAMINATION OF TWO WRITING CONFERENCES

To offer more insight into the conference process, I'd like to offer a play-by-play of two actual conferences I experienced. In the following pages, you will read through a somewhat typical writing workshop, beginning with the closing of mini-lesson and goal setting, and then flowing into writing time and writing conferences. Following this, I will offer some reflections on these accurate accounts of conferences I had on this day, in hopes of putting some of the previous chapter's advice into perspective.

The Mini-Lesson

It's a Monday afternoon, and we are finishing up our mini-lesson on structure in poetry. We focused on the purpose and use of line breaks and have been examining how shorter and longer lines affect the feel and flow of a poem. It's early October, and students are beginning to become comfortable with the process of analyzing a piece together and making writing goals based on our discussions and personal discoveries. As the lesson comes to a close, I can already see several students scribbling down their goals in anticipation of their writing. I've also noted one student who isn't jotting down their goal and who was quiet during the mini-lesson. (Student-watching during the mini-lesson creates the round of conferences to come.)

To get their attention back to me, I yell our class Call and Response with enthusiasm.

"Class where you at?"

"Give me one-mo-ment," they chant back.

"Where you at?"

"One-mo-ment HUH!" They drop their pens and pencils and whack the floor with a unified thump.

"I want to hear three great writing goals today," I say, smiling as several hands shoot up. This was not the case in September.

I call on one student. "What's your writing goal today?"

Gathering her thoughts, she glances quickly at what she wrote and then back to the poem still projected on the board. "I really liked how the first and last line of the poem are the same. I like that structure."

"Me too!" I say, excitedly. "What did we call that again?"

"Parallel structure?" she responds.

"Yes!"

She beams. "Yeah, I like that a lot. I think I can use that in the poem I started on Friday. I want to do that."

"I love it. Can't wait to see your work."

Other students who were still struggling to think of a goal jot down her ideas into their journals. They know this is, in part, why we share goals aloud. Sometimes we need help thinking of a good purpose for our writing, and getting ideas from other writers is what great writers do. They also know that this is how we stay accountable for our work.

The hands shoot up again and I call on another student. "What's your writing goal today?"

The boy called on is the joker of the class and likes to get attention with his responses. "I really liked the short lines in this one. I think I want to use short lines."

His friends nearby snicker quietly.

"Oh yeah?" I say. "What about the short lines do you like?"

The boy thinks for a moment, and then says, "I don't know. I think it makes it easier to read. I think I can write like that."

"So you're going to use this as your model text then?"

I say the term *model text* specifically because I want them to use that language in their thinking. We aren't quite there as a class yet, so I will continue to use this term as I echo their thinking. Eventually, they will begin to use it themselves.

The boy agrees, and I ask for one more writing goal. I scan the room and try to find a balance to the goals we've heard. So far we've heard a strong goal, a decent goal, and now I want one that shows a weak goal. I want to do this for two reasons—first, to hopefully help model how to strengthen a weaker goal and second, to see who might need extra support in the coming conferences. My gaze falls to the boy who was quiet during the mini-lesson. I can see that he wrote down a goal, so I feel comfortable calling on him even though he didn't raise his hand.

"What's your writing goal for today?"

He looks at me sheepishly and shrugs.

I love these moments. Starting as early as day one, I show students that shrugging gets them nowhere. I will wait until the end of time for an answer. It's in this wait time that I really get to see the student process the question. It can be uncomfortable, but being uncomfortable is far better than learned helplessness. I make it less intense by smiling and genuinely showing that I want them to have an answer, rather than using this time as a punishment. It's not his fault he doesn't have an answer, but I need to support him in being able to find it or verbalize why he doesn't have one. Both are great moments for growth.

It takes some time, but eventually he says, "I don't have one."

I nod. "Didn't you write one down?"

He looks down and shrugs again. "I just wrote what he said about short lines, but I don't like that one."

"Hey!" the other boy said in mock offense. I let it go and continue discussing with the student.

"Ok," I say, "was there anything that stood out to you in this poem?"

Another pause, but a shorter one. "I like how the poem is split into three paragraphs."

"Three stanzas do look nice, I agree."

Like I did with the term *model text*, I affirm his thoughts but with the proper vocabulary. This process leads to greater vocabulary acquisition because it's used in context.

"Do you think you could try writing a three-stanza poem?" I ask him.

"Yeah."

"How would you word that goal?"

A few kids raise their hands, but I wait for him to process and write it down. After a few seconds he reads what he wrote. "I want to write a three-stanza poem."

"Yes!" I shout in excitement for him. "Fantastic goal!" I look around the room and straighten up. They know what phrase is coming next.

"Alright class . . ." I pause for dramatic effect. "GO WRITE!"

Conferring Begins

Students skitter this way and that with their journals in hand and find their places. Some go to their tables, some find a comfy chair in the corner, one or two sit under a desk, and some stay on the carpet where we sit for mini-lessons. I watch as they go, mentally taking notes on who is eager to start and who might be less than inspired. I can always judge the effectiveness of the lesson based on how quickly students get into writing, and this one appears to be a good one. Most students have already started in just a few seconds.

Before I get up, I set the tone of the class by playing some modern music of my own via Pandora (not too loud and set to clean songs only), grab my iPad for notes, and begin making my way around the class. The music sets a nice tone for students without headphones and adds just enough background noise for small disruptions to affect fewer students. Students who prefer their own music are welcome to have their headphones, as long as they aren't wasting too much time selecting songs or staring at their phones.

I don't start conferencing right away. Rather, I walk around and see the class begin to work. Some students are deep into a piece, and some are staring at blank pages. A few are sharing their pieces with each other, which is a good sign that our writing community is growing into something bigger than just a class where we write.

After a moment, I find my student who was struggling in the mini-lesson visibly struggling to begin writing. He is slumped back, eyes glazed over, and he's avoiding eye contact with me.

Not surprising.

Without missing a beat, I sit down with him and begin my first conference of the day.

Conference One—Success and Progress

"How's writing going?" I say as I open my iPad and get out my Apple Pencil to jot down the notes of our conversation. I choose to write notes rather than type them because I have found that students feel like they're being evaluated far more if I type. I take notes on everything said—putting everything I can on the page, just like I ask my students to do. I try to model that the distance between the words we say and the words we write is shorter than we would believe. Generally, students find talking easier than writing. I try to forge the connection as much as possible.

The boy shrugs and slumps further down into his chair—the tell-tale sign that he is disengaged from his writing right now. I remember his goal, but I ask him what it was anyway to start our discussion on something more than a shrug.

"To write a three-stanza poem."

I jot this down in my notes. "So how do you think we can start doing that? What's the first step?"

He shrugs.

"You don't know?" I say with an exaggerated tone to try and get him to show me some energy. It works a little. "Come on, what do you need to start?"

"An idea?"

"Sure. What else could you start with?"

In a previous mini-lesson, we discussed what we can use to start a piece with. We listed things like mood, ideas, topics, purpose, and even emulation of model texts. By asking this question, I'm formatively assessing if he retained that information.

"Purpose?" he says.

Bingo. "Yeah, we could start with a purpose. Do you have anything you'd like to write about or to anyone?"

"My mom," he says, surprising me with a quick answer.

I write that down in my notes. Again, this subtle visual of turning thoughts into words on the page will eventually transfer to him and my other students. Sometimes seeing the process of selecting words and writing them down is half the battle.

"Your mom? Why?"

He gestures to the poem we used in the mini-lesson. "It reminded me that her birthday is tomorrow."

I write that too. "Oh, and you think you could write her something for her birthday?"

"Yeah, I think so."

"I think that's a great idea. Do you know how to start?"

He shrugs, but he has leaned forward to his paper now and picked up his pencil. Good sign.

At this point, the conference could become too much of me and not enough of him. I could easily start guiding his thinking too much, essentially stealing the power away from his piece. I don't want to do that. I want him to own his work because he will care about it far more in the long run and invest more authentic energy as we progress through the writing process. So even though there is more to discuss about his piece, and I can tell he's probably going to flounder in starting, I bring the conference to a close at this point. Now that I've got his brain working and he has a goal to focus on, I can leave him to do the heavy work of figuring out what to actually say. As his teacher, I want to take him just far enough so that he can begin to see the path, but I want him to walk it. That's where the learning happens.

"I love this idea," I say as I write it down so I can reference it later. "A three-stanza poem for your mom's birthday. I can't wait to see where this goes."

I smile and walk away, leaving him to work on his own. I'll check on him a final time before the class is over to see if he makes progress (unless he calls me over before), but for the most part, I'll leave him to work on his own. My goal in workshop is to get students thinking and working, and then leave them be. The point of workshop is to work!

Conference One Reflection

Overall, this conference was very solid. We developed a bit more rapport. I learned that he is close to his mom—at least enough to write her a poem. We worked off of goals that spawned from the mini-lesson, and the student was left with an authentic writing task crafted mostly from his own interests, with a small push from me. If all goes well, he will work, struggle, revise, edit, and possibly change focus entirely as he works through his piece and consults with me more. Each conference will lead us to different goals and purposes for the day. Each conference will open up new avenues for instruction and guidance. He will develop as he needs to as a writer, because everything I push for in those conferences is in response to where he leads. If he shows me that he needs more help with structure, grammar, or spelling, we will work on that. If he shows me that he struggles with getting words on the page, we will work on prewriting strategies. If he shows a clunkiness in language, we will work on creating a flow within his piece. If he needs to talk about his mom more to figure out what to say to her or about her, I get to learn more about him and help him learn how to pick words, phrases, and ideas from his own descriptions to use in his piece.

The excitement found in conferences comes from the unknown. I did not know that I was going to talk about his mom and guide him to start that kind of poem, but I did. This process repeats all throughout the workshop, leading me to teach not just one mini-lesson, but potentially over twenty in one class period!

If that sounds tiring, it is, but in the best way possible. Once a writing workshop is in full swing and students are producing work that's authentic to their desires and interests, it becomes exhilarating to sit with ten different students in a class and home in on ten different teaching points. At the end of a heavy conference day, I am drained beyond belief, but spiritually, mentally, and professionally filled up with so much joy that I can't wait to get back into it the next day.

But what about when a writing conference goes poorly? What does that look like, how do you respond—and what can you learn from a difficult conference?

Conference Two—Learning from a Difficult Conference

After leaving my previously struggling student, I immediately spot another student reading a book in the far corner of the room in our big purple chair. Even though I tell students they can break up their writing with reading (because reading makes us better writers), I still hold writing time to be sacred. We have already had our reading block where students are allowed to read their books of choice, so she should be writing unless she is finished or looking for a model text or inspiration of some kind. We set this boundary and general rule early in the year, because I want the writing process to feel natural. Writers don't write 100 percent of the time, so I don't expect students to, but some students hide in their books as a way to avoid doing writing at all. That's when I step in and figure out what's wrong.

I make my way over to her to see what's up. I crouch down next to her. "What are you reading?"

Sheepishly, she shows me *Ghost* by Jason Reynolds.

"Oh, I didn't know you picked that up! I love that book a lot."

"Yeah, it's pretty good. I just started it."

"Just now?"

"Yeah . . ."

"What made you grab it?"

"I don't know," she says.

I see that her journal is closed, so I pivot the conversation a bit. "Well, keep me posted on what you think. I bet you'll love it . . . How's writing going today?"

"I couldn't think of anything to write about."

I jot this down in my notes. "The poem we read didn't make you think about anything?"

"No."

"Hmm . . . it happens," I say, trying to figure out what question to ask to get her to talk. I can feel the conference waning in energy already. Not a good sign.

I quickly look at my notes of a conference we had together last week. "Are you still working on your short story?"

"I got stuck."

"Do you mind showing me? Maybe I can help out."

She gestures over to her closed journal. "I ripped it out last night. It's on my bedroom floor . . . I think."

"Ah," I say. I'm mildly defeated and I can see we aren't making much progress. I can also see out of the corner of my eye that three hands have gone up from students who are requesting conferences.

"Well it sounds like you're having some struggles today, that's ok. Can you do me a favor?"

"Sure."

"Read right now, but I want you thinking about ideas to write about as you read. You might get something from that book, or maybe an idea will pop in your head at dinner. Tomorrow I'm going to talk to you first, and I want to hear about what you've come up with. Sound good?"

"Yeah, I can do that."

I jot down this plan in my notes, her watching from her seat. I then offer a high five and move on to meet with other students in the class.

Conference Two Reflection

So . . . what is there to learn from this difficult conference? A lot. First, I now know that she is at least somewhat of a reader. She didn't have a reason for picking up *Ghost*, but she did that rather than looking at her phone or talking to another student, so that's a small win and piece of observational data that will inform how I approach her in the future. I add this to my notes as I walk away from the conference.

Second, I know that she is mildly self-conscious about her writing. When students tear out their work, it usually means that they don't see it as valuable enough to keep, or they are afraid they will be judged too harshly. These emotions stem from past school experiences where the student's work wasn't valued or supported enough—a problem many students come to us with.

Third, I know I need to take on the role of extreme supporter in her writing life. This is when academics take a back seat for a bit. For example: I could have approached her and talked about structure, since that was the focus of the day's mini-lesson, but she was so far from actually writing that forcing that talk wouldn't have done much for her. For this student, I need to get her to write and care about what she writes. I need to show her that her work matters before I ever try to get her to think critically about it. Writers can fix anything that is written, but they can't fix a blank page.

My plan with this student is to follow up the next day and see where she is at. If she has an idea or plan for her story, great! If not, I might approach her with some more questions to help generate ideas. All it takes is one idea to get a student like her going, but finding that one can be tricky. It can get frustrating as the days go on and little writing has happened, but I want to resist pushing her into topics or pieces she doesn't care about. If it takes two weeks for her to find one great idea to write about, then that two weeks was worth it. Just think about all of the choices, thinking, processing, and connecting a student has to do just to get to the point of choosing a topic and writing on it! As far as I'm concerned, as long as I can be sure the student is thinking, processing, and mulling through their work mentally, that is just as good as actual writing.

Good thinking leads to good writing. Knowing this, I am trying to model and guide student thinking with strategic questions and discussions. This is quality teaching and work time, even though nothing tangible is being produced. Thinking isn't something you can put a gold sticker on, but it's the most valuable act in a classroom.

This is why note-taking is so important during conferences. Not only will it allow me to keep track of who I've talked to and what has been said, but also it will allow me to speak to the *quality of thinking* from my students in the form of anecdotal notes. Every district official and school leader wants to see evidence that students are learning and progressing—and teachers should too. Those notes will help me speak to the progress students are making, even if they are writing less than the desired amount. Furthermore, those notes will help me in remediation if there is a problem that needs to be addressed or concerns that crop up about the student's efforts in class.

It's All About the Student

In the end, conferences are about the student and what they need next. They're about the process of listening—truly listening—to the needs of an individual student and being able to offer just the right amount of input to get them moving forward.

A conference is not used to teach five things. It is used to find one thing a student is doing well, and move them further into mastery by providing the conditions for them to do so. A conference is also not the time to cover a student's paper in corrections or remarks on grammar. Writing all over a student's paper in a conference, or even during grading, takes the ownership away from the student and gives it back to the teacher. If we want them to put their hearts and souls on the page, we cannot directly or indirectly take ownership over their papers. Instead, find ways to leave brief notes for students to reference later such as leaving a sticky note, jotting them on the blank side of their journals, or better yet, having them write their own notes from conferences, so that they own every aspect of their writing space.

Conferring Is the Fuel for Beautiful Work

I could write endlessly about my experiences in writing conferences. The stories students have to tell are astounding, inspiring, and at times, heartbreaking. I learn so much from my students in these one-on-one talks, and I believe they learn about me too. I listen more than I talk, but I also share with them. I share when I connect to something in their lives or respond to one of their stories with my own. Often, we spend our conferences laughing with each other or coming to a new understanding of one another. And it's in this process of a genuine back-and-forth that ideas are found, and great writing is formed.

Great rapport with students yields detailed, passion-filled writing in all genres. When students feel safe to talk about what matters to them, their writing blossoms, their work ethic increases, and they begin to work. Not because it is school, but because that work is meaningful to them. As a plus, as you ask deeper and deeper questions about their writing, students begin to think with those questions in mind, and thus elevate their writing further before they come to you. Students begin thinking like writers and about the potential audience. They begin to think about *purpose*, which is the difference-maker in writing.

If I hadn't developed rapport with my student by sitting down with her and discussing how she felt like she gave so much to the world and got little in return, she wouldn't have written "Imagine."

Imagine

Cyanna Boone

Imagine loving someone
so much that
YOU go without,
to make sure
THEY go with.
Imagine loving someone
so much that
you feel as though
YOU need THEM,
and can't live without them.
Imagine being stuck
in the dark, lonely, and cold
world, with nobody
to guide YOU
to the bright
shallow light.
Imagine being crumbled, with NO ONE
To put YOU back together,
and cherish you
and all of your flaws forever.
Imagine not being
able to put YOURSELF
back together, that you need
SOMEONE else's hand
To make YOU, YOU.
Imagine being there for everyone,
and NO ONE to be
there for YOU.
What a crazy thing
I can imagine.

If I hadn't sat with my student and taken a deep dive into how he views overthinking, he would have never written a piece about how the clouds (thoughts) can block the real beauty of the world.

The Setting Sun
Leandro Guerrero

Hidden in a sea of darkness
I can barely make out the setting sun
I can only catch a glimpse
A glimpse of the mesmerizing reds, purples, oranges
Mixing and twisting into a magnificent array of colors
Engulfing the land with a radiant heat like no other
But instead there is only one color
A cold
Barren
Color
That seems to have no end
No excitement
No joy
No happiness
Nothing
After a while it clears up
Only to show a pitch-black sky

If I hadn't sat with my student and discussed that her uncle has Alzheimer's disease and how that makes her feel, she would have never written "The Difference."

The Difference
Micaela Martinez

You have to wake up not knowing where you are, or who you are, or who are the people around you. You just have to live like that.

It has been 17 years since the last time my dad got to see you and you can't even remember him. You can't even remember your own son.

It's not your fault. I just can't wrap my head around the fact that you can't remember anyone. I can't wrap my head around the fact that you have to live like this forever, and you can't do anything about it. And I can't do anything about it.

And when you wake up tomorrow, you won't know the difference.

CHAPTER SEVEN
UNDERSTANDING THE SHIFTS OF A WORKSHOP

The writing workshop is a world of changing weather, growth, and evolution. It can be volatile, changing in minutes, and it can be calm and predictable for several days. Newer workshops all experience similar weather patterns, while more-experienced workshops change in other ways. Knowing this and looking out for these changes is key to not becoming discouraged as your once-vibrant workshop goes through a stale period. Fear not, it is all a part of the natural order of things.

New Workshops

There is an excitement at the beginning of a brand-new workshop. Everyone's collective energy brings about a magic that naturally lifts the lesson and work being done in the classroom. Students are excited about the rare but rightful freedoms being offered to them in their class, and they gravitate to the joy that freedom brings. Seeing this, the teacher is equally excited (and most likely nervous) and brings even more positive energy to this experience.

Since many students come into the workshop having little experience with writing authentically, early lessons are a bit broad and high-interest, so that teachers can hook students in and get them to enjoy class. These lessons inspire students to write early on, setting things in motion quickly. For a teacher who has never experienced the opening of a workshop, this early period can feel like going to sleep in the dead of winter and waking up to spring bursting in full bloom under the noon sun. It can even be jarring at first to see how much students want to work and how diverse and engaging their writing is.

In secondary classes, especially in grades that foster the transition from elementary to middle school, students will enter workshop with furor. They will write quickly, often in the forms taught to them in elementary, and look forward to showing you what they have done. Students who aren't used to writing for authentic purposes will stare at their pages and stay relatively quiet. Some may talk or get off task, but for the most part, they can be easily redirected, depending on your experience with classroom management. Some students have had the opportunity to write freely in the past and others have not. Accept this without judgment, and focus on getting to know your less experienced students to get them writing.

In these early days, as long as your students are enjoying your lessons and dipping their toes into writing, everything is okay. Remember that you are the expert in your class. As you learn more and more about the writers in the workshop, use more of what gets them engaged in your mini-lessons. Keep it short. Model the standard process of mini-lesson, practice, goal setting, invitation to write, and conferring from day one, and you will be right where you need to be come week two.

The End of the Honeymoon

Putting a specific time frame on when the first shift in workshop will occur is difficult. It could happen on day three, seven, or eleven—but the wind will change, and the clouds will roll in. The honeymoon period will end, and the real work will have to begin.

It's important to note that this may feel like a failure at first, if you aren't used to the shift. Students who once started writing quickly now say they have nothing to write about, get off task, or dawdle in their seats. The once-quiet students who tried to hide from you will actively seek distractions now, either with other students or on their phones or Chromebooks, whichever is available. Already talkative or active students will feed off of this and become the wanderers, the instigators, and the students whose names you learn first because you say them so often. These behaviors are your clue that students are ready for more targeted and meaningful lessons.

Frustrated teachers will walk away from a day or week of this and say writing workshop is a failure and immediately want to tighten up the structure of everything. They will think that students can't handle so much choice or freedom in how they approach work and then rob them of this right in their education.

Resist.

Remember: Making choices is rigorous work. It is difficult to do well. Depending on the grade level you are teaching, students may come to your class with a decade or so of never having to make a choice about how to approach a piece of writing. Resist the urge to punish them by taking choice away, or worse, giving them a false choice offered as real freedom. Both are equally damning to a workshop. The first removes their right to own their education. The second is a lie, which erodes trust in you as a guide for their work. Both are the antithesis to empowerment.

The floundering of a new workshop is normal, and it happens to everyone. Hopefully, if you are at this point, you have been conferring with and learning about your students through the honeymoon phase, so you know what they need. Examining as much of their writing as possible and taking copious notes on what they say, think, feel, and believe is extremely valuable as you transition to deeper mini-lessons.

The conference serves as data gathering for what needs to be taught. What common areas of opportunity are there in your class, and how can you address them?

Maintaining Momentum by Understanding Writers

As you make the shift to address what your students need now, the workshop will begin to pick back up, and this time, it will gain momentum. But students' individual and collective writing struggles won't simply disappear. The clouds will return. That's why being forthcoming with students about the struggles of writing daily and how you yourself manage (because you are writing, too, right?) is so important.

Many workshops that fail to soar are often held down by the unaddressed stress that comes from writing in general and the myths about writing that uphold that stress. To maintain momentum, we must think clearly about actual writing behaviors that appear when writers write for their own purposes, rather than for the grind of school.

Most writers do not sit down and write for a solid thirty minutes or more. They stop. Stutter. Erase. Flail. Listen to music. Glance at social media. Text. Make a joke with a friend. Go to the restroom. Stare out the window. Rather than expecting students to write for extended periods of time without stopping or experiencing mild distractions, encourage them to behave like writers do in the real world. Embrace the freedom and messiness that comes with it.

Writers do not outline everything they write. They don't revise every line or have pure editing phases. They edit, revise, rewrite, and draft all the time while working on a piece. Being open about this takes pressure off of students to follow the standard model of writing in school. Writers work on drafts until the draft works, period.

Writers do not consistently write pieces that are better than their last, much like each sentence written in a book is not better than the last. Some are and some aren't. Writing progress is not linear, it is a collection of volume, effort, and patience. Understanding this qualitative data and why it's so valuable is key to pushing back against the quantitative-obsessed systems we often work within. As time goes on and students write more, the sum of their production will show the growth they are making, and not only you will be able to speak to it with actual examples over time, but students will as well.

Writers change topics and stop drafts if they aren't working for them. None of us have time to write about ideas that don't inspire us or bring us back to the page. Writers finish drafts and move on. They also put away drafts and come back to them, if they choose. Sometimes words don't come, or they stall, or what needed to be said that day has been said. Instead of forcing them to write consistently through writing time, which is the urge, encourage them to use their time differently. They can read, revise, or if your class is at a certain level of self-management, they can help other writers and confer with them.

Writers should have the freedom to say what they need to say with the words they need to say it with. In other words, if a student uses the phrase, "I can't take this shit anymore," and we respond with negativity about their language, we rob them of the tools writers use. Are there appropriate and inappropriate uses of certain words and phrases? Of course, much like a research paper is written differently than a personal narrative or song. However, if a student uses certain words or phrases within the right genre and for a valid purpose, limiting their word choice is just another "school" approach to writing. If you teach secondary and find swearing to be deeply offensive, I have one thing to say to you: People curse. Sometimes no other word captures that specific emotion. Besides, it's satisfying. Try it.

Writers borrow lines to get started. Skilled writers use them as models, altering them to fit their needs. I don't know where I would be in this book, for instance, if Tolkien had not written the words, "This book is largely concerned with hobbits . . ." which gave me a model for my own version, "This book is largely concerned with writers . . ."

Writers do not show everything they work on. Being forced to show someone their words before they are ready to do so will make even the most well-off writer waver in the honesty they bring to the page. Forcing sharing at any point, unless there is good cause (such as fear for the well-being of a student, for example), is another needless restriction on the workshop. Let students write and own their writing. When we force them to show us what they are writing at all times, we subconsciously tell them that what they are writing isn't theirs. Instead of being a negative force this way, ask students if you can see what they are working on, and let them know they have the right to say no. Eventually, they will say yes, and your connection with them as mentor and fellow writer will be deeper and far more meaningful.

This book cannot possibly list every do and do not exhibited by writers, so it's best to become one yourself and watch what you do. The more you are a writer, the more your approach to the writing workshop will be more relevant to them. This means that when your workshop begins to wane, and it will, you will know what it's like to lose inspiration and be more valuable to the writers in your space.

Finishing

After a few weeks in a decent flow of work generation, teachers will often begin to get anxious and want students to start actually finishing pieces, not just writing. Teachers will walk away from a few weeks of workshop feeling good about the writing, but noticing that students are changing pieces or topics often or simply not finishing what they start.

This is natural, and because we are in a school setting and not in a utopia, it is perfectly reasonable to want to see your writers finish and publish pieces. Again, this is where being a writer pays off. Writers know that sometimes you just have to push past the doubt on a piece and work until a draft is completed. Oftentimes, what we find is that it is better than we thought as we were writing it. Sometimes it's horrible, but the practice of finishing a draft is a net positive no matter what.

Deadlines can help motivate many students, but do not rely solely on them. Drafts are done when they are done. Forcing a student to finish a piece because of an arbitrary deadline made by you will only force them to rush and learn less in the process. Don't offer freedom to just strangle it for the sake of the gradebook. Use the deadline as a nudge, if it's useful. For many it won't be, so develop a focused approach to keeping students honest through their output by conferring regularly about progress and goals rather than grades.

Continue to keep note of which writers are floundering the most, and which ones just need a little nudge, and talk with them often. Be encouraging on their stronger pieces and push for them to finish a draft and publish. Once they get a taste of finishing something and the feeling of accomplishment that comes with it, they will get hooked on the process.

Once the majority of students publish in a particular round of writing (usually coincided with your grading periods), the workshop will experience a lull. Distractions will creep in more and students will flounder. As this happens, embrace this period and ramp up your mini-lessons with texts that are high interest and inspiring. Use pieces that connect with the students you have in your class, not premade lessons made by a teacher somewhere else with students who aren't yours. You will know them very well by this point and will be able to strategically target what you choose for mini-lessons to get them fired up to read, think, discuss, and write.

Rules of Thumb

When writing is stalled or slow in the workshop, make your mini-lessons broader, more accessible, more engaging, and more inspiring. Focus on giving writers fuel for their own work, driven by the knowledge you have of them. Curriculum guide or not, if writers aren't writing we aren't getting anywhere. Give students what they need and the writing will pick back up.

When writing is going well, make the lessons more focused on skills and techniques used by writers. Too much inspiration can hinder progress by sending students off chasing a better idea. Constantly assess the climate of the workshop and make mini-lesson decisions accordingly. The ebb and flow of the tide of productivity will work itself out.

Ultimately, it's all a cycle. Every part of a workshop: the mini-lesson, model texts, discussion, practice, worktime, conferencing, and publishing all work together to create ever-changing shifts in the workshop and the lives of the real humans in the room.

Educators know that students cause the change of tone in a space just as much, if not more, than the decisions made by the teacher. It all connects in writing workshop, and it's on the educator to be vigilant and positive about how to support each element in a way that keeps students rightfully empowered in their work.

Writing workshop teachers are always asking questions, both to their students and to themselves:

- What is going well in the workshop? What's going badly?
- What do my students need to see to inspire their next piece?
- What genres do we need to examine next to inform our writing choices?
- What reading are we doing to keep our minds fueled with ideas and examples?
- What am I, the teacher, doing to get in the way of students writing freely and passionately?
- How are the habits of school creeping into authentic writing and the purpose for that writing?

As long as you are working daily to meet the needs of the writers and embracing the ever-shifting nature of the writing workshop, progress and achievement will be the norm in your class.

CHAPTER EIGHT
THE GROWTH OF WRITERS

Writers grow by writing. It's really that simple. When we keep writers writing, we see growth. A writer is not always better than their last piece, but they become a sum of their work. Voluminous writing keeps the mind thinking about writing and trains the mind to be ready to write at specific times. Don Graves said, "If students don't write at least three times a week, they are dead." Any teacher who has tried and failed at making writing happen only once a week has seen the *dead* Graves is referring to here.

If writers know they are expected to write every day at a specific time, they will slowly become more alive with ideas, and their ability to put words down on the page will grow exponentially. This ability leads to more volume and more time to confer. It leads to more chances to try new things, exploring ideas, emotions, and feelings. It leads to more time working with words and how to use them to create meaning for others.

As time, practice, and support intertwine repeatedly throughout the workshop, you will see students grow. The pieces they write at the beginning of the year will be entirely different in finesse, power, and meaning than the pieces they write at the end of the year.

Writing Journals

Tracking student growth is a primary goal of the workshop teacher, because it highlights why the workshop process works. Final pieces that have been published and added to the students' writing portfolios are a stellar way to track growth, but so are the students' journals. Having a specific journal, folder, binder, or online resource dedicated to all the drafting students do in your writing workshop will be a living record of how they have grown as writers in your space. I have found the most success with physical journals in my own room. Students can see it filling up over time, and there is something magical about having a book that is dedicated to you, your words, and your life.

Be religious about these writing spaces. Encourage students to not tear out or delete unfinished or imperfect drafts (they will want to). Encourage them to move on to the next page if they are stuck on a draft or want to quit the piece they have lost passion for. Inform them that this isn't a mandate, it is an honoring of their work and their words—which is true. We might not love what we wrote yesterday, but what we wrote—that we wrote—is worth preserving. We used our voices and our minds, and that is a profound act of existence.

As a teacher concerned with growing the writers in your care, you will use these journals (or whatever space you decide on) as the record of their evolution. As the year hits natural lulls, say around winter break, spring break, and the end of the year, the journal will be available as a record of how much growth has truly occurred—not only in the final drafts that live and thrive on the walls of the class and in their portfolios, but also in the messy parts where authentic writing battles the world for meaning and purpose.

Encourage your students to keep their journals with them always. Many teachers want to store these in the class so they do not get lost, to which I respond confidently that students will take care of them if they believe in the words they write in them. Empowered writers protect their work and look at it often. Accidents happen, of course, but the accident of training students that their voices ultimately belong tucked away in a crate in the classroom is worse than replacing a journal that got ruined in the rain.

Three Writers and Their Growth

The following examples are from three writers who grew over their time with me in the classroom. Their writing has been preserved to be representative of the work they published.

As you read these pieces, pay attention to how they changed over time, especially how their topics matured, and their control of language became laser focused. You'll be able to see how these students' writing changed during our time together with much greater clarity than a standardized test could ever show.

Ratatoe and Cheeseamo   Viviana Castro—Piece 1

Once upon a time there was a rat named Ratatoe. Ratatoe was in a crew named the Six Musketeers, the members of the crew were Cow, Sassy Steph, Berry, Bumble Bee and Potatoe Joe.

The Six Musketeers had a mission and that mission was to sneak into the most famous cheese factory in the world. The name of the factory was Vivi's Cheese Factory. There was to sneak in very quietly and grab as much cheese as they can.

Ratatoe and her family once tried to sneak in but the owner caught them and almost killed Ratatoe's mom. The Six Musketeers already knew when the owner went to lunch.

When it was time to sneak in everyone followed behind Ratatoe because she knew the way inside. Everyone was scared because they might get caught.

Once everyone was inside the factory they were so surprised of how much cheese was in the factory.

"Everyone get as much cheese as they can," said Ratatoe.

Potatoe Joe and Bumble started looking around and found a cart they hurried to get it and came back.

"Look we could put the cheese in here," said Bumble Bee.

"Good job Bumble Bee," said Ratatoe.

"I helped her too!!" said Potatoe Joe.

"OK, good job Potatoe Joe and Bumble Bee," said Ratatoe.

Everyone was getting a lot of cheese because they knew it was their only time that they could sneak into the factory.

Ratatoe noticed a cheese that looked really delicious it was yellow, very shiny and really big. Ratatoe went to get the cheese.

"You're mine now," said Ratatoe.

"NO!! Please don't eat me, I have kids of my own," said Cheeseamo.

Right before Ratatoe took the cheese he heard the door open.

"THE OWNER, RUN!" said Berry.

"WHERE?" said Cow.

Everyone looked at Ratatoe because they thought he knew the way out.

"I don't know a place out," said Ratatoe.

"WE ARE GONNA DIE!!" said Sassy Steph.

"Wait, I will help you get out," said Cheeseamo.

Everyone stopped freaking out and looked at Cheeseamo.

"But you have to do something," said Cheeseamo.

"We will do anything, just help us," said Bumble Bee.

"What do we have to do?" said Ratatoe.

"Just don't eat me, and I will help you," said Cheeseamo.

"OK, fine I won't eat you but hurry up and tell us the way out," said Ratatoe.

Cheeseamo jumped out of the shelf and started leading everyone the way out.

"Are you sure this is the way out?" said Ratatoe.

"Yes I'm sure," said Cheeseamo.

"Ok," said Ratatoe.

About ten minutes later they were out of the factory.

"Thank you," said Ratatoe.

"No problem," said Cheeseamo.

"Well it's time for us to go," said Ratatoe.

"Bye and thank you," said everyone.

"It's fine I've helped many people sneak out, I'm pretty used to it," said Cheeseamo.

The Six Musketeers went on my way and Cheeseamo went the other way and happily ever after.

The End

Forever.   Viviana Castro—Piece 2

Depression is amazing. Don't you just love when it hits you? Don't you love when it makes you cry? How it makes you cry. How it makes you think of how lonely you are and how perfect you aren't.

Depression hits you hard, those are the best days in life. You cry your eyes out and think of how un-perfect you are but people never find out what's wrong with you, why? Because you're just showing a façade.

Depression becomes your best friend. The more it comes, the more you get close to it. When it comes you become happy that your friend is back, and you'll be sad when it leaves. It never wants to leave you. You guys stick together.

Forever.

My Everything
Viviana Castro—Piece 3

I'm addicted,
to the burn,
to the pain,
to the tears,
everything it brings that hurts me.

I hate the pain, but
I'm addicted to it.
It's like I need it,
like I can't survive without it.

It's my happiness,
my past,
my now,
my future.
It's the air that I
breathe,
the ground I walk on,
the people I know,
and the strangers I pass by.

It's my everything.

The Angry Flamingo

The hairless cat sat on the window ledge
Staring out over the river's edge

He had only one fear
Seeing the other cats with hairy ears
He went out one day
He even put on sun spray

He still thought he might burn
All the other cats, acting so stern

There were many cats at the beach that day
He was just gonna put out a towel and lay

He just lie there all alone
When he was done, he went home

He looked in the mirror and-OH-
He looked like an angry flamingo

He decided to never go out
For the rest of his life, he'd sit and pout

SILENCE

tap, tap, tap, tap

The rhythmic pitter-patter of the rain hitting the window and sliding down dejectedly, making room for others.

The air rages. Dancing through the leaves in the trees, leaving them reaching.

The vivid blue flashes across the deep, inky sky, lighting up the ground.

A low rumble chases after the light, rattling the windows and walls. Terrifying small children.

The steady downfall becomes a weak trickle, then a humid, sticky silence.

Normal   KMO—Piece 3

I try
to have a normal conversation
like a normal person
I try
to be like them
I can't be
like them
I can't be
normal

I try to be serious
and I can feel it coming
I hold it in
as best I can

it feels
like I'm about to burst

an urge
begging to escape

then it happens

my head jerks left
pulled by a chain
that only affects me

I try
to ignore it
and carry on

and keep talking
as if
everything was
normal

as if
I was
normal

their feet shuffle
their eyes shift

I stop
talking,
moving,
breathing,
everything

they walk away
giggling
as if
the conversation ended

I stumble back
my knees tremble
then collapse
so I'm balled
against the wall

my breathing
now shallow and shaky

my head falls to my knees
and my tears make their way
down my red cheeks

I just wanted to be
normal

Flower

Hailey Rosales—Piece 1

I get to brighten up each spring with beautiful colors.

Everything smells so good that everyone

comes to visit me every time

to take pictures.

But then

I'm

dying.

My

leaves

falling.

I'm

brown

for

months.

Until it starts to

bloom and I get to brighten

up each spring with beautiful colors.

Everything smells so good that everyone

comes to visit me and to take pictures with

me and the beautiful colors around them and joy.

My Song

Hailey Rosales—Piece 2

"Cause I, I'm in the stars tonight."
It makes my mood go up
Instead of going down
And brings the joy on my face.

I can't believe this song
Is making me move, and
That everything around me
Is so great that I
Forget about it all.

THE GROWTH OF WRITERS

Even though I can't really dance—
I still get up, move around like a
Monkey that doesn't even know what
They're doing.

Now that it's getting towards the
End, I still want to
Replay the song over and over again,
Until I need to do my work.

Dirty Windows   Hailey Rosales—Piece 3

Over the years
I have seen my true self
and how people change
and how you see
the truth—

But it's stupid to try to
ruin my life with the lies
They are like
Dirty windows, I see
through them and see the
real you that you try
to hide

I loved you, I love you so much—
but you ruined it all, my
Heart sank when you tried
to take me away from my
home

Do you really want
to hurt me more than
you have

You pretend like
nothing happened and think
I will be the same like I
used to and that's never going
to change even though we
are related—

But things have changed
and no matter
what you try to do
nothing is going to
be like it used to
be

All three of these students were with me for two years, and you'll notice that they began as most sixth-grade writers do: with childlike writing. Fun and whimsy, usually narrative focused. As the year progressed and then faded into another, their writing became far more personal, empowered, and potent in their approach to big, emotion-packed pieces. You'll notice the transition to poetry as well. We use poetry in class to focus on lines, sentence construction, and practice with homing in on big ideas worth exploring. But more importantly, and as I said in the introduction of this book, every piece presented here was freely chosen to be written. None of this was assigned. When students see the power poetry can command, and the freedom it offers as they work on honing their ideas and language, they tend to pick it most often to write within. Poetry provides a natural chunking mechanism for homing in on structure, word choice, and purpose. Once poetry is demystified in the workshop, young writers grow to love it.

The students I teach have to write essays for state tests and curriculum demands just as much as many students do across America. They meet the demands of those practices far more easily after having written twenty poems to completion, rather than writing four essays over the course of the year.

And unlike data derived from standardized tests, the poems students produced show their personal growth as well. Most importantly, these students were able to understand and articulate how they'd grown.

In Their Words

At the end of the 2019–2020 school year, one of my students reflected, "This year, I have definitely changed a lot in my reading and writing. In elementary (all the way to fifth grade) I HATED reading. I wouldn't finish a book all year (unless it was a *Magic Treehouse* book), but this year I think I've finished fourteen or fifteen. I used to like to write on my own, but I disliked having a prompt (which was always). I still don't like writing to a prompt, but I have more freedom now, so I like it much more. I've grown to understand why authors do certain things and how to advance my writing, and I'm very proud of that."

Another student said, "This year I have grown to be a better writer. I think the main reason for this is because I got to read and write what I wanted. I found this helpful because this made me be able to be passionate about the things I am writing and reading, therefore making me happy to write and read. I have grown the most in my writing with the words I use and how I make my writing sound. I like the fact that I got the chance to write about problems in the world and other important stuff instead of just writing about something someone made up for me to write about. I am the most proud of the way I put the words in a sentence to make the sentence more powerful."

Echoing this, a student added in their own reflection, "I believe I have grown in both subjects because this year I got to read and write more than I ever had. This year I got to write what I wanted and express my feelings, and I believe that really helped me get better in writing. I get more expressive in my writing and I've loved to write poems. I never thought I would like it, but I did. It's a way of expressing your feelings in a really short writing. I'm proud of how far I've come in writing and I wish I would've written more poems. I will definitely write poems when I go traveling this summer. Thank you Chastain for helping me discover my passion (for now)."

Personally, I love the added "for now." It has a hint of begrudging acceptance of how writing has changed this writer's life. I could share many more of these testimonies, but they all share similar sentiments. Being freed to read and write what they want made even my most-resistant readers and writers embrace the process and come to enjoy it. It allowed them to grow into the writers they always had the potential to be.

CHAPTER NINE
GRADES

Whenever I am presenting for teachers or responding to direct messages and emails from the *Teach Me, Teacher* or *Craft & Draft* podcast, I am inevitably asked about one unavoidable topic: grades.

"Where do you get your grades from?" teachers ask.

"How do you assess student writing?"

"What kinds of tests do you give?"

These are loaded questions, and the answer you take to heart will largely be dependent on where you teach and what mandates you must follow to keep a paycheck. Because of this, I will be as frank as possible. Decide where you fall on the spectrum of grading philosophy.

Traditional Grading

On one side, you have the traditional model of grading. Students do assigned writing, teachers take in this work, mark it up with a pen and highlight all the errors, and put on a grade that is supposed to represent student mastery of content. Grades are often given throughout the writing process—for having an outline, for example, or for each individual draft or step in the editing process.

It's quite possible that you were educated in English classes that subscribed to this grading model. This is a top-down approach where the teacher has all of the power in the class and the students have very little. They are workers who get evaluated often and can suffer dire consequences for falling below a preset standard. This model puts student deficits first and accomplishments second. It fits into the box of school because school often fetishizes quantitative data while ignoring qualitative data. The school system loves simple answers to complex problems. That's why multiple-choice questions about grammar and highly restricted prompted pieces thrive in this model—because they create the kind of quantitative data that is easily translated into data charts and spreadsheets.

Feedback Model

On the other side of the spectrum, grades take a back seat. The class becomes a place of feedback, rather than of pure evaluation. The teacher sits with students daily to discuss what is working in their writing and why. Teacher and student dialogue about pieces as writers. The student keeps control of their piece. They decide when it is done by choosing when to trash a piece that isn't working or publish and move on to something else. When evaluation does occur, the students evaluate their own work with the teacher in an honest conference about a piece or several pieces. These evaluations serve as a holistic examination where purpose, growth, style, and mechanics all play a role in deciding what level of content mastery has been met.

It's quite possible that this level of freedom in grading sounds too good to be true, or maybe it sounds unwieldy and imprecise. Both are assumptions made up of a distorted view of what writing is.

Most aspects of writing are subjective. How well an author demonstrated an argument, explained a topic, expressed a feeling, used figurative language, and crafted a plot (to name a few) are subject to the perceptions of the evaluator. This is the obvious reason why a book beloved by many can have just as many detractors. Just because one person does not enjoy a piece of writing does not mean it is any less worthy of merit. Just because someone loves a piece of writing does not mean that it deserves the praise being showered onto it.

An empowered writing workshop takes the realities of writing into account. Writers write for a variety of purposes and publish work that varies in quality and accomplishment. Writers take on passion projects and work on pieces that might highly connect to them, but not connect to others. They also write in a way to capture more readers, possibly simplifying prose or vocabulary to do so, and they write to innovate on old ideas. A grading system that comes from the top-down approach or one that centers grades as the primary reason to write will never be able to account for these facts about writing, and thus limits student voice, sabotaging freedom and equity in the process.

As the educator, facilitator, and most-experienced writer in the room, you have to decide what role you want to play.

The Spectrum

The more grade-centric your class is, the more power you take away from students. When you remove authentic purposes from writing (there's very little authenticity to grades), you remove voice, passion, and soul. You create an artificial landscape of winners and losers. Writing becomes a high-stakes task where punishment or consequences loom over the writers' heads.

The more feedback-centric your class is, the more power you give to students. You encourage them to explore, take risks, and use their voices for authentic purposes. Their souls come out and play in the world of words and creation. By lowering the stakes of writing, it flourishes in many different shapes, colors, and styles, mimicking the diversity of the young people sitting in your class.

Writers who only write for a grade are writers who will likely never understand what writing is and what it's for. Writing teachers who fail to give students what is rightfully theirs—the freedom to use their voices and express themselves—are teachers who are failing their students in a way that has far greater consequences than a fifty in the gradebook.

However, there is a spectrum. Most likely, where you fall on the spectrum will be mandated by your campus or district. Currently in my own work, I am still responsible for grades, data reports, and tests, but I do not keep these in the forefront. In fact, I try to push them as far as possible out of the view of students.

Due to the system I work in, and the system my students and their families are used to, I set clear requirements for the workshop. An example of these requirements looks like this:

- Students draft *roughly* three to four pages a week in their journals.
- Students confer at least once a week, but they can do so as needed.
- Students publish at least one piece in the grading period, but they can publish as often as they like. After winter break, students will publish at least two pieces a grading period.
- Pieces published in the grading period will be used for student-led evaluations with the teacher to assess growth in content and serve as a snapshot of ability in that moment. All pieces published within the grading period will be considered in this dialogue and will make up their test grade for that period.
- Students maintain a journal that represents their body of work in the class.
- Students maintain a writing portfolio with all of their published work in order of publication, with a record of their writing—the title of the piece, genre, and date finished—at the front of the portfolio to help track volume over time.

While most of the workshop is focused on feedback, there does come a time when grades have to be entered and evaluation has to be discussed in most schools. Over time, I have created an approach to grading that I believe honors the freedom and rightfully empowered workshop described so far in this book. Below I describe how the workshop and its expectations translate into grades and assessments. This process is not gospel. (I tweak it every year, to some degree.) It's just one example of how I have found a balance between an effective and open workshop and the standard life of school we must contend with.

To begin, the requirements above get entered in the gradebook as number grades, as per my district's mandates regarding grade requirements. I support the grades with my conference notes, pictures of students' work, and the publishing process itself, meaning drafting, revising, and editing. Students maintain writing portfolios where they keep published work and add to it as often as they publish.

For every requirement listed above that is met, the student receives a hundred as a daily grade. If they miss any aspect of what has been listed, their grade lowers accordingly. In my own class, this is done by tens, with a minimum grade of a fifty. (I do not believe in zeros in the gradebook.)

To put this concretely, if a student is supposed to draft three to four pages of rough draft a week, but on our Monday check only drafted one page, that student would lose twenty points for that check. However, I do allow students to justify not meeting the requirement for pages written. For example, if they have evidence to show that they were working deeply on revisions (which rationally lowers page production), then the deduction of points is waived.

This is not a top-down approach to grading, because the expectations and structures are set to honor student voice and time, and they have the freedom to explain the work they are doing that might not fit within a neat box. None of this is a gotcha. Students understand from the first week of class that this is what is expected, and why this is the expectation. They understand that in my class, they will have a minimum of thirty minutes of uninterrupted writing time a day. Three to four pages of rough draft is more than achievable, especially if they are working on shorter forms of writing, such as poetry. Contrary to popular belief, freedom does not mean the diminishing of high expectations, it is the realization of high expectations in action.

Test grades are derived from published pieces and the writing portfolio. Rather than students handing in pieces I assigned, they choose pieces they believe represent their learning and work the best, and we evaluate and discuss the pieces together. Before the discussion, students fill out the following form on their own.

Writing Reflection

Use this section to tell me about your piece. This is how you justify the grade you think you should get, so be clear and detailed!

Be sure to talk about:

- What you are proud of
- What your purpose was for writing the piece
- What mini-lessons and/or model texts you used from class
- Anything else you'd like me to know about your piece

_____

_____

_____

_____

_____

_____

_____

_____

	1: Needs Improvement		2: Approaches Standard
	3: Meets Standard		4: Masters Standard Student

Student			**Teacher**	
	Mini-Lesson / Model text usage			Mini-Lesson / Model text usage
	Purpose for writing the piece			Purpose for writing the piece
	Grammar and genre conventions/structures			Grammar and genre conventions/structures
	Evidence of the writing process			Evidence of the writing process

Students tell me about their pieces in writing and then self-evaluate their work based on a point scale. Each point lower is five points off of the final grade. Together, we discuss the piece and all the nuances of the writing. At first these discussions are driven by me, but as the year goes on and the writers become more confident and skilled at speaking about their writing, this process becomes an empowering act of students pointing out their own learning and progress. They become empowered by the fact that they control their work and take part in the evaluation of it.

There is also freedom embedded in this process because it allows students to justify why they might have done something that would otherwise warrant a lower grade. For example, they might not have used any model texts or mini-lessons from class in their piece. While I want them to do this, because it ensures that they are always working toward incorporating what we are learning into their writing, I also understand that inspiration comes when it comes. If a student feels passionate about a piece and believes that it's their best work, I want that to be honored in a class focused on them. Allowing for discussion surrounding a grade is an acceptance that grading writing, outside of mechanics, is entirely subjective and imperfect. Understanding this is essential to a rightfully empowered workshop.

With that said, the quality control built in is the teacher side (right) of this evaluation. As the educator, I build in a space for me to push back on or encourage students' evaluations of themselves. Sometimes this means pushing for a student to honestly consider the four (perfect rating) they gave themselves for a piece with no periods present, but mostly, it means I am raising their level of awareness about the great work they do. In my experience, I find that students grade themselves lower than I would if it were just my decision. The best part about this structure is that I get to be their supporter and encourager, helping them see all the greatness in their writing. Eventually, they do this themselves.

As a final act of reimagining how grades are obtained in class, I tell students that writing is not done for grades. Writing is done for writing's sake. We exist within systems (in school and beyond) that demand we evaluate our growth over time, but that does not mean that we only write to fit within such systems. Students may write five pieces that do not fit into an A as represented on this form, but they can write as much as they want to achieve that A. In other words, students can keep publishing until they have perfect grades across the board. They can also publish many pieces just because they love them, and a few that get them the grade they want. This teaches that we write for different purposes and audiences, without being punitive to their desires. For prolific writers, this system honors their body of work, and for struggling or slower writers, this system empowers and focuses their efforts into manageable goals. For writers who need more time, care, and attention to achieve growth and mastery, I even allow them to miss certain deadlines for publishing, counting their work-in-progress as their grade. If I am diligent in keeping evidence of learning and tracking progress, I can differentiate between students who aren't meeting goals because they are deciding not to meet them and students who simply need more time within their own learning journeys.

At the end of the year, students evaluate their work over time and reflect on their own growth in class. They examine aspects of their work, such as their biggest accomplishments, and consider where they would like to see their writing go next.

Students Are Not Deficits

When students know that their grades are not based on their deficits but on the work they put into their writing, they produce more. Teachers and administrators often misguidedly think that students will not work if a grade isn't being assigned and ignore how little students are actually writing. Using grades as coercion makes students write less, not more. Compliant work is work done only to stay out of trouble.

When we take these constraints off of kids, they spread their wings and explore. They fall in love with writing and the writing process, not because of school and a love for the content, but because the writing workshop becomes a place about *them*. The writing workshop might be the only place they go all day where they feel like they can be who they are—expressing their thoughts, ideas, feelings, and emotions—and not feel like they will be punished for doing so.

What a gift we can hand students—the right to their own education.

As teachers, we get to decide what runs our class. Every educator has limitations put on them by a variety of sources. It's not an excuse, rather, it's a call to be innovative and make professional choices that benefit the ones we serve.

CHAPTER TEN
BE AN ADVOCATE FOR YOUR STUDENTS

Grades are not the only evidence of conventional school systems' emphasis on control. In fact, most school systems (not the people in the systems) despise freedom. They are designed to standardize everything, in the vain hope of proving growth and mastery in the exact same increments with predictable results.

A rightfully empowered writing workshop operates within an equitable framework that aims to serve each writer in the ways that they need to be successful. It does not have the goal of securing the same results for every writer, outside of growth, because every writer has different goals. Each one has a different purpose for writing, and that will lead to vastly different outcomes. The students within our classrooms deserve an education that fits their needs and supports their interests and unique experiences.

Teachers bear on their backs the weight of this heavy system and all of the nuances that go with it. They go on producing data so that the powers that be can stay in charge, while doing their best to protect their students from this system's most pernicious effects.

Unfortunately, this insidious system does eventually reach the minds of young people. As a consequence, students begin to believe that their voice is only as valuable as their grade, and that their education is just an endless proving ground where they have to perform for assessment after assessment in hopes that they can be considered proficient or on-level by artificial measures created by people who don't know them.

This process is entrenched in the public school systems. Politicians on the Left and the Right have made it worse. From No Child Left Behind to Race to the Top, there is no shortage of bad policy that attempts to strip teachers and students of rightful empowerment. That's why we must do all we can to advocate for our students, to show the powers that be that freedom, not control, results in the learning young people need to succeed—as students and as human beings.

An Uneasy Balance

Many of you reading this are probably used to constantly balancing what your district and government want with what your students actually need. You read about a rightfully empowered writing workshop and think it's nice but calculate a hundred reasons why it won't work. You think about growth measures, testing data, curriculum alignment, and readiness and proficiency standards. You think about data walls, data meetings, and data binders. You think about every single thing that is in your way, keeping you from serving the young people in their space.

The solution I offer is a shift in focus—a shrugging off of the world of systems of control and an embracing of the world our students and writers deserve. This world is sustained through advocacy that takes into account what students truly need to become rightfully empowered writers.

How to Be an Advocate

Teachers and administrators must be partners. There is often an *us vs. them* mentality in this relationship, and it isn't helpful to anyone involved. In my experience, there are administrators who understand why an empowered and free workshop is valuable to students, and there are administrators who are resistant to the concept. Even so, I have yet to run across an administrator who does not want what is best for kids and their families. Taking this into account is important because it humanizes those administrators who may be wary of a process that pushes against some of the traditional models of school. If we want to effect change in a large way, we must invite in and work with our colleagues and administrators. Being the renegade teacher is something many have done because they feel like they have to, but being a positive force and building understanding between administration and yourself will yield far more rewards in the end.

If you are working with colleagues or administration that are resistant to implementing a rightfully empowered workshop, you have to be the one to educate about, and thus advocate for, what kids really need. When you walk into a data conversation or sit in a professional learning community, you have to be ready to not just speak about the empowered work you are facilitating in your workshop, you have to be ready to give context and show what that looks like and how it is directly contributing to the deep and meaningful learning of the students in your care.

Don't shrug off a failing world and replace it with nothing. That world will just end up back on your shoulders, and probably much heavier than before. Replace what you drop with something truly inspiring and beautiful. Come ready to defend your decisions with actual student work and information on why you are doing what you're doing, and why it is working.

Below are some suggestions for how to be the most powerful advocate you can be.

Be Meticulous

Keep track of your progression of mini-lessons and the texts you use as models for your students. Note which texts were particularly powerful and how they brought about changes in student writing. Be able to share how a specific text or craft lesson changed the writers in your space for the better.

Individualize your notes, giving each writer their own folder, tab, or section in your app or device of choice. Track how many times you meet with each student and keep copious notes during conferences. Take pictures of student work in progress, of notes made, and of what you added to student thinking to move them forward in their work. Pay particular attention to applications of mini-lessons in student writing, but do not force a connection just so you'll have the data to share. A piece needs what a piece needs, and it only hurts the writer to force the issue. If a mini-lesson never shows up in student work or thinking, you know that mini-lesson was not effective for your writers and can discuss this with your team and administration. (This is also important to note during the coevaluation phase at the end of publishing.) Being able to say what didn't work is just as valuable as saying what did. Don't be afraid to admit failure. Don't be afraid to admit success.

Highlight Student Volume and Growth

Let students publish often, at their pace, and speak to the volume students are producing. As students publish, they will get addicted to the process and want to do it more. Volume equals progress in writing. The more you do it, the better you get. Speak to this by honoring the many words your students write. If we can put red, yellow, and green dots on a data wall, we can put the imperfect pieces written by young writers up as data too. They want data? Show the real work students are doing.

Advocate with Facts

Educate others about the simple fact that writers do not grow on a linear scale or in the same ways as one another. The piece they write this week is not necessarily better than the piece they wrote last week. Try writing every day and see if you are consistently better than the last time you sat down with the page. Furthermore, one writer might grow in command of word choice but struggle in structure, while another may grow in mechanics and still struggle with focus. The traditional school system is not designed to honor this nonlinear progression. It doesn't fit the business model many educational leaders subscribe to. Capitalism has been wonderful in many ways, but it has also seen to it that we constantly look at data and expect numbers to go up, regardless of industry. Even so, the development of human beings is not an industry—school is not equivalent to the business world. It is a fallacy to equate education to business. Human beings are not capital gains. Human hearts are not profit margins. Human souls cannot be inserted into a return-on-investment spreadsheet.

Advocate with Evidence

The best advocacy is a preponderance of evidence in your favor. Do not fall into the trap of advocacy without evidence. It will be an exercise in frustration and despair. Being able to track when a mini-lesson was given, how students used it in their chosen work, how growth is happening daily in conferences, and how this all ultimately comes out in their final pieces will elevate every aspect of your talks with those who might be resistant to the rightfully empowered workshop.

The System Can Wait

Once you've put everything in place to be a powerful advocate for your students, do what needs to be done to keep you in line with your job and its expectations. You know your situation and school. Fit in the testing and the data collection. Put up your data walls. Do what is asked, but put students first. Rather than starting with the oppressive systems, subvert them by doing what is right, and fit in these other pieces as required. There are pieces to the accountability behemoth in the United States that, if ignored, can close your schools and cost people their jobs. Without a doubt, this is a bane on administrators, teachers, and students. These realities are not forgotten in this book. But as you create a workshop that rightfully empowers every student, you will find new ways of implementing these aspects into your class. Rather than finding time for students to write, you will find the time to get the multiple-choice test done and the data turned in. Serve your writers first. The system can wait.

With that qualifier out of the way, fight systems not people. Most educators in administration and in the classroom are well meaning and passionate. Blaming them for being in-line with the system as it stands and dedicating your efforts to being combative is fighting the symptom, rather than the cause. It's the same as blaming kids for not completing lifeless work assigned to them—systems have a way of shaping how we behave. Understand this and realize that not every-one is willing to or capable of addressing and fighting outdated and oppressive systems. While some people may even defend the systems criticized in this book, being combative with the people you work with ruins potential and current work relationships, degrading the effective-ness of your campus in the process. Even when we disagree with one another, we must work in ways that leave room for an eventual coming together. Disrespectfully disagreeing gets us nowhere in the work we must do. Respectfully disagreeing leaves us room for much more.

Be an agent for change and collaborate with colleagues inside and outside of your building as often as you can and in as many ways as you can. You will face educators and administrators who are hes-itant to change and possibly hostile to ideas about creating a right-fully empowered workshop. Working with them over time, even in small ways, will be more effective in changing systems than creating battlegrounds where no one wins. There is strength in numbers. Alone we are capable of a lot, but together we can be the revolutionaries our students deserve.

The system will change, and it will be the brave educators who aren't afraid of backlash that lead the way. Oppressive systems are only as effective as their punishments. If their punishment loses its hold on their subjects, the system collapses. The rumblings in the system are already happening. The future is bright.

CHAPTER ELEVEN
TRAUMA INFORMED

The close work we do with students gives us valuable insight into their growth as writers. This work also reveals to us the whole person and the whole worlds they encounter, both in and out of school. Students don't come to school only to learn. They come to gather socially and meet with friends. They come for the regular meals and safety most schools can provide for several hours a day. They come for the mental and physical services that keep them healthy.

With that said, schools are severely underfunded for the number of services they provide students and their families. In 2016, The Education Trust reported that students outnumber counselors 464:1. This problem is exacerbated when you look at the abysmal statistics for schools that predominantly serve students of color and those who come from low socioeconomic backgrounds. The report also says, "A school counselor who serves predominantly students of color has to serve thirty-four more students every year than a school counselor who serves fewer students of color, and twenty-seven states are shortchanging either their students of color, students from low-income families, or both."

Consequently, rightfully empowering the voices of those students most underserved by the school system has never been more important. When you remove oppressive pedagogical choices and quit assessing student work through a deficit or standardized model, you take part in the single-greatest educational revolution of our time.

Voices for Change

Once you begin running an authentically driven and rightfully empowering writing workshop, students will begin using writing for a variety of purposes. Many will think aloud and wonder. Some will dream. Others will reflect and pour out their souls onto the page, bleeding their experiences out in ink.

Many students have not had prior opportunities to reflect openly and honestly on the challenges they face. There is power in expressing these experiences, and there is pain—for the teacher and students. There is also healing and redemption.

Writing is uniquely powerful in its ability to release the burdens of the soul and lighten the heart. In its most honest form, it is a way of making the realities of our lives seem more manageable, even though they may be heartbreaking. It's as if piecing together words and sentences allows us to piece together our fractured feelings, memories, and experiences into something that resembles wisdom and understanding.

Providing a space where members of marginalized communities can put words to their authentic experiences is a gift that spawns revolutions and change. When we open up our world to the sound and plight of people who have been calling for change over the course of decades, we begin the healing of a broken society.

Empowering communities to write and express the true grain of their experience should be a primary focus of the writing classroom. These pieces become anthems and manifestos of change in a world that is in desperate need of it.

More Than Angst

For teachers, creating a space where students can openly express their most painful experiences can be a weighty experience. Those of us coming from a place of relative privilege may not be prepared for the level of trauma present in the communities we serve. Many teachers feel this weight and immediately move away from authentic writing. They get scared of honesty and truth. Some educators cower from the pain students are feeling and immediately begin pushing it into the corner so school writing can continue. I have seen some even downplay the pain of students and say that it's just a phase. It's just teen angst.

It's not, and it's time we accept kids for who they are. Our jobs are too important to hide from the truth. The writing workshop is where truth comes to light.

The worst response we can have to students' honesty in writing is to silence them by making them fit into a box designed by a system that was never meant to empower them. It is their right to be able to express their pain, their sorrows, and their tribulations in the ways that they deem fit.

The workshop isn't the place to worry about content appropriateness for school. It's the place to ask is this honest, is this true, and is this the best way it can be said.

Anxiety   Aubree Martinez

It's like my mind gets put in a
different place,
and I just want to yell for everyone to please give me space.
I begin to feel like this hopeless monster.
My words can't even form
without me having to gasp.
I can't escape.
I can't run away, because even if I tried to,

I'd have nowhere to go.
Nowhere to stay.
My brain feels swollen
from all my overanalyzed thoughts.
All the tears down my face,
a never ending stream.
And then suddenly I'm all choked up.
Just my luck.
I can't even do something
as simple as
breathe.

Ghost Kisses   Jaqueline Rivas

They tell me that you are gone, but I don't believe them. Your parents flood the house with tears, screaming upward for you to come back to them.

I sit in your bed waiting to hear the door open, to see your face peeking through as you send me kisses in the air.

In the note you left, I feel you sitting beside me, saying everything is going to be okay. I can feel the warmth of you beside me. I can almost feel your arms behind my back as you try to hug me so I can calm down.

At the end of the day, I know the sun won't reveal itself again, and neither will the clouds stop crying.

I've Lied Before

Viviana Castro

It's true I've lied before.
In fact, I've lied too
many times.

I've lied to my
friends, family, teachers,
but I've lied to all
of them the same way.

What way? You're probably wondering,
I hide all my feelings, especially
the bad ones.

They always think I'm
OK, because I tell them
that, but I'm actually
fucking hurting inside.

I feel like I should
kill myself and that
they hate me.
Why can't my
feelings go away?

I just can't deal
with them anymore.
Why can't I stop
lying?

Forever
Angelina Cardenas

I'll miss you forever . . .

I'm starting to forget your voice, the things you told me, and the way you made me feel. You made me so happy. You were my father figure. I make myself busy so I won't think so much about everything, and how I got the call. . .me reacting to it being you. . .you were gone.

Everything I do reminds me of you. The little things you taught me and did with me. . .I will forever and always miss you, always and forever.

The Real Me
Anonymous

Everyone thinks that the real me is obnoxious, but I'm not. I modify myself to match the description. You don't know me. The real me is calm. I'm not myself around you because the real me can't be himself. If someone found out who the real me is, the expectations would heighten. We can't handle that, I'm sorry. So for now, you deal with me, not the real me, the one you created. Hope you like what you've done.

12 Words
Xavier Garza

I'm begging you.
Please come back.
I need you.
I love you.

12 words I shall never forget.
RIP Veronica.

Students feel so much shame in their pain. Give them the freedom to be honest. Give them a space that is safe so that they can begin to heal from what has hurt them or at least begin to process the hell they have gone through.

In a rightfully empowered classroom, you will have students who express themselves in ways that will make your heart ache. You will have students who release their pain, suffering, and trauma onto the page. If a student reaches a point where you believe that they are a danger to themselves or those around them, as an educator, you must report it. You must also report if a student has been hurt or is being hurt. Please understand, internalize, and follow your district's procedures in such cases.

Because of its freedom, the rightfully empowered writing workshop can reveal harmful issues with students before it is too late. Even though the writing workshop is founded on trust, and it may feel like breach of that trust to report something, reporting harm and potential harm is the clearest promise a teacher can make to a student. It would break the trust of the writing workshop if we didn't report when a student is in danger. Trust comes with safety, and we owe it to those around us to protect one another, especially those who need it most.

Overcoming Empathy Fatigue

As a teacher constantly welcoming such a high level of emotional honesty, you can begin to feel empathy fatigue. Seeing so much pain day in and day out can make your eyes gloss over to the experiences that are very real for your students. It's a natural experience—it's our mind's way of protecting itself. It's also just the nature of teaching and working with many students. Our day-to-day actions in the classroom can be like zoning out while driving a car.

If you begin to feel this way, take a break from conferring or reading pieces. Reset. You can also revitalize your focus by asking questions to the student about what they want from their piece, what their focus is, and what their goal is in including something specific in their piece. Asking questions to the writer you are working with, especially if you start to feel drained or glossy-eyed, allows you to be inspired by the person, not the task. The task of meeting with students can become just another thing you do, but refocusing on the person is a reminder of the importance of the work in the first place.

The writers you work with are young people beginning to learn how to process the many atrocities they will see and experience. How many students have suffered unnecessarily because they were not afforded even the slightest guidance from wiser individuals? You don't need a degree in psychology or to be a counselor to be a good person to someone who is experiencing pain. You don't even have to be someone with answers—you just need to be someone with a little more experience who can shine a guiding light. Sometimes that light comes in the form of a mini-lesson that helps them make a path in their own thoughts, and sometimes it's an extended conference to help a writer through the dark wood they woke up in.

Regardless, as a teacher, professional, and passionate supporter of young people, you are equipped, or can be equipped, to be the light your students need.

Step Up

The role of schools has long been hotly debated by educators, politicians, and the communities we serve. Many believe that schools shouldn't offer the many services listed above. Many believe that it isn't a teacher's job to be so many things for kids, especially without adequate pay.

In some respects, these people are right. Teachers should teach. Schools should be funded with counselors and professionals who can guide students through trauma and pain. Teachers should be paid more in America, especially if society is going to keep asking them to do more without providing the training or funding to do so. Unfortunately, these battles are still being fought every single day in the political sphere. So what? Do we just ignore the needs of our students until then? Do we decry the unrealistic expectations being put on us, or do we offer what we can in the hope of relieving some pain for our students? Do we resist the call that has been unjustly put upon our underpaid shoulders, or do we show up for our kids and offer everything we have?

This is our calling. This is our job. We serve young minds and offer them the tools they need to navigate their lives.

The rightfully empowered writing workshop gives students room to be honest about their challenges, cope, and evolve within a safe environment. The rightfully empowered writing workshop takes away as many restrictions on the mind, heart, and soul as possible, allowing students to be themselves without consequences—not only growing in their mastery and skill in writing, but also growing as people.

For teachers, it can be scary to allow so much freedom—to see the pain come out of students who you never would have guessed could harbor such stress—but it can also be affirming. When students begin to take control over their pain, rather than being controlled by it, teachers begin to realize this isn't just education, school, or assignments anymore. It is life. Full, breathing, messy life, and it rightfully belongs to our students.

CHAPTER TWELVE
WRITEFULLY EMPOWERED

If I could wish for anything, it would be that this book catalyzes your thinking and practice in the same way a rightfully empowered and equitable workshop has been a catalyst for change in me and the students in my care. Seeing nonwriters change into writers, writers home in on their voice, and suffering students turn into students who can manage emotions and channel them into pieces of self-actualization and advocacy has been life changing for them, and me. Sitting among such change and raw human power day in and day out is what makes me love the job. I deal with all the garbage teachers deal with, not because I am a glutton for punishment, but because I am baptized in the spirit of creation every single day in the rightfully empowered writing workshop.

There is nothing like it, and I hope that when you close this book, you understand that this is not only possible, but something each of our students deserve to have access to. Education has become synonymous with terms like *testing* and *data*, while acts of creation and becoming a better human have been pushed to the side. This dichotomy has reached a fever pitch in today's world as public education continues to be attacked and questioned, and as educators and administrators push for systems that no longer oppress but liberate. Many special-interest groups call for an educational system that is sterile and standardized, while educators fight for the support that students actually need to be successful.

Indeed, if we were to help students navigate their own hearts and minds more than we help them navigate Plan-Do-Study-Act charts and data folders, I believe our world would begin to heal.

This work is not about supplying answers to students; it's about rightfully empowering them to find their own. Even a little truth found in this work is worth more than any number generated from a standardized test.

This work is not about curriculum, the game of school, or the gradebook; it's about offering a flame to our young students and letting them find their own paths to build in this dark world. They will go places we never dreamed of. They will solve problems we can't conceive of. They are the future, and we can either force our own images upon them or understand that it's their right to create new images for what their lives and society can be. We can either force them to be like one another, or embrace their differences and allow them to be unified in their uniqueness.

The final pieces collected here are the honest words written by middle school writers who have been rightfully empowered and who therefore write fully empowered. They explore ideas and thoughts that connect to their hearts, minds, and spirits. They use the written word to express themselves and to understand the world around them. Some pieces were inspired by mini-lessons, difficult and good conferences, and what students read, but all the pieces were written because they needed to be written by the writers who wrote them.

They didn't need an assignment to do this—again, no student writing present in this book was assigned.

They needed a classroom designed from the ground up to support what is theirs by rights—voice.

Dark Waters   Viviana Castro

When I go to sleep
My feelings come out
Into the darkness
Into the place they
Belong.

They flow around me
Like dark waters trying
To drown me into
Thoughts nobody likes
Hearing.

Under all the dark
Waters there is a
Monster pulling me
Down, he never lets me go,
He is addicted to the power
He has over me and to be honest
I'm addicted to the pain he gives me

And as I wake up
The waters fade away
But I still feel his power over
Me.

Shadows   Viviana Castro

I wake up thinking
I'm free
Thinking the monster
Is gone.

Turns out he has
Locked me in a

Cell with him,
I try to escape
But he holds me back.

He needs me,
Needs to hurt me
And I need him too,
I need him to give me
The pain that I like feeling.

I hear his heavy breathing
I feel him watching me
I want him to take me back to the dark waters
I need him to drown me in the waters.

I need him to baptize me
In his shadow.

In a Moment   Viviana Castro

How much can happen in a moment?
Happy and nervous
Changes to the feeling
Of thinking I'm gonna die
When I hear people screaming
And see them running. I don't
Know if I should run with them or
Hide, all of a sudden I'm getting pulled
By my friend, seconds later a random lady
Tells us to hide and that we will be safe but
I think what if I die tonight. My tears flow down
My cheeks, the tears aren't for me, they are for my family
The family I didn't say "I love you" to,
To the family I will probably never see
Again.

To the family-
To the dad
To the mom
To the sisters.

Dad you are always
Working and never spend
Time with us but now I
Realize that you work hard
For us to have whatever we
Want and need.
Mom all those times you scream
At me about my grade being low
I build up with anger but now I
Realize it's for my own good, like you said.
Mayerly, I always hate it when
You give me those sloppy kisses
But now I wish those kisses would
Be the ones on my cheeks instead of these tears.
Valeria, you are so young that
All you do is cry for help but now
I wish I was hearing your cries instead of mine.
I wish I would've done everything right.
I wish the life that I lived didn't leave me wishing in my last moments.

Tanks   Leandro Guerrero

The sound of tanks moving on the gravel roads
A scary sight, indeed
But that is not what I'm scared of
I've fought tanks before with just a rifle and a grenade
What I'm scared of is what's in front of these tanks
Polish Women
Burned
Beaten
Hungry
No, starving
Used as shields
Everyone around has dropped their weapons
Everyone horrified and in total shock
Now we have a choice
Surrender or retreat

Empty   Xavier Garza

I haven't eaten in weeks.
I have scars on my wrist.
I walk around hoping
no one notices.
I just want to escape.
To get away from everything
and leave it behind

I'm empty like the blank walls
that encase me
and my mind is scattered
like the trash on my floor.
Every day the walls close in
closer and closer.

YOU
Angelina Cardenas

I still think about
you here and there.
I can't make my thoughts
go away.
I want to go back,
back to when you were here with me.
One look at you
just brings me back
to everything.
I still can't push myself to believe you're gone . . .
I miss you. . .you were my happiness
and forever will be.
You and you only had this special scent
and the best hugs.
I look at you once
and everything is just OK again.
I can't have that no more,
and I don't.

WHY
KMO

We are just little specs
In the universe

We think
That every action is important
That we have the ability to change everything
That one mistake makes you a bad person
That if you want to get somewhere in life,
you have to be a "good" person

But in the end
None of it matters

We will all die
And it will have all been for nothing

We go through all of this pain
All of this work
All of this life
And it was all for
Our satisfaction

It doesn't matter
Because it will all go away
Along with life

I sit there and wonder why we are here. I mean, the world is going to end one day, and there is nothing we can do about it. Everything we've done or will do, will go to waste.

I realize that, yes, one day the world will end, but while we are here, why not make the best of our time. One day you won't be here to do that, so do it now, while you can.

Why were we put here if one day, we will die anyway?

There must be a reason, so just be excited and find it. It might be whatever makes you smile so keep that with you.

Maybe it's to make someone else smile, so why not smile along with them?

I wrote this to give myself a positive to all the negatives that go through my head. It doesn't really have a closing statement or paragraph but there is a reason for that. Someone might say that you can't be sad about something because there is something else to make you happy, but I don't think there always is. I felt that if I closed this out with a reasonable statement, it would end up saying something like "so be happy," and I don't think that would be very appropriate for this. There isn't a positive to every situation, so I left this to be up to you, the reader, to decide how you feel about this. I think that sometimes you *should* be sad. I personally have more ideas and think more when I'm upset, but when I'm happy, I find the positives to *some* of those thoughts.

Your turn to decide how you feel.

Falling Apart   Joselyn Martinez

You hear
screaming
yelling
crying.
You find
your parents fighting
again
again
and again.
They call you down
because they
have to tell you something . . .
They tell you that
They
Are
Separating.
You repeat that in your head
Over
Over
And over again.
You have tears coming down your eyes
One
By
One.

You feel
Hurt
Depressed
Gloomy.
You feel like your
Whole
World is
F
A
L
L
I
N
G
apart.

Schedules Cyriss Taylor

6am. Roll out of bed. Put on clothes. Grab my stuff. Get in the car and head to the courts. I spring to life as I see my friends playing, and I join them. We start playing. . .serve. Backhand. Forehand. Forehand. Backhand. Another. Finally we're finished and the bus arrives. We grab our things and the bus takes us to school. We go to second period, then third. Fourth. Fifth. Sixth. Seventh. Finally eighth. I walk home. Do the homework that I rarely have. Eat dinner. Shower. Sleep, and do it all over again.

Stay Away Makayla Dennis

Stay away,
it causes
a lot of pain.
Your loved ones
wondering . . .

what did they do wrong?

As they are visiting you behind bars

crying their eyes out

wondering . . .

What got into your head?

Your friends?

School?

Or even your own thoughts?

Through the bars

we see you,

but do you

see yourself?

Us?

Father   Adraiya Hill

I can't stand you. Every lie is another reason for me to hate you. Your manipulation works on me because I tend to give you the benefit of the doubt. It's like I know what you're doing and what you're saying isn't going to happen, but at the same time, I believe you, because I convince myself I want you to do what you say you're going to do. I know you won't, and that's what hurts. Your words are like fire. They're pretty from a distance, but when I get close. . .I get burned.

In My Head   Adraiya Hill

I need a hug

To be honest

I'm kinda sad and it's gotten to the point

Where if you touch me for too long

I get sort of teary eyed

I feel like I need a good cry though

So I can get a lot of the stress

And the negativity out of my system
I tend to hold in a lot of my emotions
To where it gets to the point
Of a borderline mental breakdown

I don't really like opening up to people
Especially since I always get mistreated
In some way

I don't like worrying my parents
With it either so I just keep it to myself
I make jokes about it sometimes
I say it's a joke, to help me cope
But I'm dead serious

They think it's a joke though
Which is the whole point I guess
I don't know if it's a healthy way
To do so, but it works for me
Sometimes

Death Upon Myself   Brooklyn Tillman

Upon myself
I wish death
Not because I want to die
I wish death
Upon myself
So that I may be reborn as a child
A child that knows naught the ways of the world
The weight of the world
The everlasting dread of the world
Nostalgia
My youth dwindles
Fades
And I face my inevitable future

And when I am old
Elderly
My skin stretched, wrinkled
As my mother's once was
And those before me
Upon myself I wish death

Straight Pride . . . Natalie R.

More than 600 LGBTQ+ members in the US have been killed
in the past two decades for loving who they love
and straight people want pride.
Children get kicked out of their homes for loving who
they love
and straight people want pride.
Gay kids get bullied and beaten up for who they love
and straight people want pride.

OK. You can have pride after
you've been beaten up for liking a girl.
You can have pride
when you've been abused and kicked out of your home for
liking the opposite sex.
You can have pride when you get arrested for
being cisgendered.

Let me know when you're an outcast for being straight.
Then you can have your pride month.
Let me know when you go out on a date with the opposite sex
and get dirty, disgusted glares from strangers.
Let me know when your parents hate your guts for loving the
opposite sex.

Then you can have pride.

Home Life
Chloe Peters

When people say
Things to hurt others
Most likely
They aren't in a good place
At the moment
They probably
Just need
A break
From where
They're at
People do things
Because they
Don't want it
To happen to them
They abuse
Because they don't
Want to be
Abused.

Tiny Prayer
Elise DeArmond

Running,
Free,
Suddenly rolling,
Down a hill.
Sweet smell of magnolias,
Stop.
Looking up,
Beautiful sky
Birds flying,
But they aren't just flying,
They're running from something,

A storm.
Running again but not for fun,
Sky turning grey,
Like God is mad at me.
Stuck.
Whole world behind me.
Nowhere to run,
But a Miracle,
A tiny prayer,
Changes everything.
Storm stops,
Everything wild ends.
All because a tiny prayer.

Everything.   Kamoria Ellis

I feel like everything
every day
Every hour
Every minute
Every second
Every   breath

I took just stopped.

Like ever since you were gone I feel like

every day is still Friday.

Every hour is still 2:00 AM.

Every minute is still 2:34 AM.

Every second is still 2:34:12 AM.

Every breath is yours, keeping me on my feet.

I'd rather stay in 3/23/2019 than live like you never left.

The Survivor
Liliana Perrin

The sun is shining
The animals are playing
The birds are chirping
The trees are standing
Tall and bold
Strong and beautiful
The sky darkens
The animals run away
The birds go silent
Humans come
Chopping every tree down
One by one
Chop
Chop
Thud
Thud
Only one remains
Standing there
Tall and bold
Strong and beautiful
And it watched
As all of its
Friends and family
Were chopped down
And carried away
Homes were destroyed
Nests were ripped apart
Animals that once lived in that forest
Now have no food or shelter
And inadvertently will die
Baby birds that will never learn to fly

Now lay on the ground
Helpless and defenseless
And that one tree
Watched it all
Wishing it could help
But it couldn't move
Its roots kept it in place
Humans built roads
Buildings
Towns
The tree always saw
Tons and tons
Of humans walk by
But none of them
Ever saw the tree
Standing there
Tall and sad
Strong and beautiful
Weeks passed
And still the tree stood there
No birds made nests
No animals played
No babies were born
The tree was empty
And still
No one ever saw the tree
Standing there
Tall and sad
Strong and lonely
Nights were longer
Days became shorter
The wind blew colder
And the tree grew sadder

Leaves began to fall

Branches began to break

Snap

Snap

Thud

Thud

And the tree watched

As humans went by

Learning so much about them

Their problems

Their worries

Their hopes

Their dreams

Wishing the tree could help

But no one knew about the tree

Standing there

Tall and sad

Useless and lonely

Days were cold

Nights were colder

Snow would fall

Branches would break

And the tree began to die

Very few branches were left

Bacteria, mold, and fungus

Started to take over

The tree's barely alive

And yet

No one saw the tree

Standing there

Sad and lonely

Weak and ugly

Useless and dying

The sun is shining

The cars are driving

The humans are talking

The tree is dying

There are no nests

No homes

No animals

No birds

And the tree finally collapses

Thud

The tree is dead

And now

Everyone

Sees the tree

Laying there

Decayed and branchless

Useless and sad

Ugly and dead

They all stare in shock

They could've helped it

They could've saved it

But it's too late

None of them ever saw the tree

Until now

ACKNOWLEDGMENTS

First, I would like to thank the students who are featured in this book and their families. Being able to not only work with such great human beings in the classroom, but also collaborate to create a book to help many others across the world is something I could have only dreamed of as a young educator. It's a reality now, and we built this together. You all put your hearts and souls into these pieces, and this book is alive because of it. This book is yours.

Second, I would like to thank every administrator who believed in the work I've championed over the years, despite all the failures I have had along the way to this moment. Not every teacher is lucky enough to work with leaders who support their staff, but I can firmly say that I have. Leeann Bartee, James Whitfield, Ross Nelson, Mark McCanlies, Jennifer Klaerner, Lisa Johnson, Jody Fadely, and Billy Neal, I would not be the teacher I am today without the support from you all.

Third, I would like to thank Regie Routman, Jaqueline Stallworth, and Evan Godwin, for reading early drafts and pages of this book. Your time and effort to help me shape *Writefully Empowered* does not go unnoticed or unappreciated.

Fourth, I would like to thank the many educators who have shaped my approach to the classroom and guided me on my journey in a variety of ways. Staci Hammer, John and Melinda Bolles, Pam Ochoa, Kate Nelson, Kelly Gallagher, Penny Kittle, Donalyn Miller, Laura Robb, Jeff Anderson, and Anindya Kundu have all shaped me in powerful and tangible ways. You are all some of the best educators I have ever met or studied from. This book would not exist without any one of you.

Finally, I would like to thank Dave and Shelley Burgess for believing in my work once again. Without your willingness to take chances on books that are a little different, I'm not sure any of my words would have ever reached the printed page.

ABOUT JACOB CHASTAIN

Jacob Chastain is the host and creator of the award-winning podcast *Teach Me, Teacher* (and author of a book by the same name) and cocreator and host of the *Craft & Draft* podcast. He is an author, speaker, trainer, curriculum writer, and teacher. He currently teaches seventh grade English in Ft. Worth, Texas, where he lives with his wife and son. He holds dual master's degrees in curriculum and instruction and administrative leadership from Dallas Baptist University.

Jacob believes that educators should push to change what it means to engage students in the classroom and improve their craft to create equitable opportunities for all students. He is an advocate for public schools and the amazing educators and students in them.

His *Teach Me, Teacher* podcast reaches tens of thousands of educators every month across the world, is a top-rated podcast on Apple Podcasts, and has featured some of the premier minds and personalities in and around education.

Follow him on social media:

Facebook—Facebook.com/teachmeteacher
Instagram—@heychastain
Twitter—@jacobchastain_

WORKSHOPS AND KEYNOTES

Jacob Chastain leads dynamic, hands-on workshops centered on reading and writing workshop, equity, and engagement. Using the experience gained from his professional degrees, work in public schools, and the hundreds of discussions he's hosted on both *Teach Me, Teacher* and the *Craft & Draft* podcast, Jacob works with teachers to not only imagine what workshop teaching can be, but also create systems and procedures that bring such images to the real world of teaching.

His keynotes draw from his experiences living among drugs and abuse and how education and teachers changed the course of his life. He also talks about the power of choice and freedom in the classroom.

MORE FROM

Dave Burgess Consulting, Inc.

Since 2012, DBCI has published books that inspire and equip educators to be their best. For more information on our titles or to purchase bulk orders for your school, district, or book study, visit DaveBurgessConsulting.com/DBCIbooks.

More from the *Like a PIRATE*™ Series

Teach Like a PIRATE by Dave Burgess

eXPlore Like a PIRATE by Michael Matera

Learn Like a PIRATE by Paul Solarz

Plan Like a PIRATE by Dawn M. Harris

Play Like a PIRATE by Quinn Rollins

Run Like a PIRATE by Adam Welcome

Tech Like a PIRATE by Matt Miller

Lead Like a PIRATE™ Series

Lead Like a PIRATE by Shelley Burgess and Beth Houf

Balance Like a PIRATE by Jessica Cabeen, Jessica Johnson, and Sarah Johnson

Lead beyond Your Title by Nili Bartley

Lead with Appreciation by Amber Teamann and Melinda Miller

Lead with Culture by Jay Billy

Lead with Instructional Rounds by Vicki Wilson

Lead with Literacy by Mandy Ellis

She Leads by Dr. Rachael George and Majalise W. Tolan

Leadership & School Culture

Beyond the Surface of Restorative Practices by Marisol Rerucha

Choosing to See by Pamela Seda and Kyndall Brown

Culturize by Jimmy Casas

Discipline Win by Andy Jacks

Escaping the School Leader's Dunk Tank by Rebecca Coda and
     Rick Jetter

Fight Song by Kim Bearden

From Teacher to Leader by Starr Sackstein

If the Dance Floor Is Empty, Change the Song by Joe Clark

The Innovator's Mindset by George Couros

It's OK to Say "They" by Christy Whittlesey

Kids Deserve It! by Todd Nesloney and Adam Welcome

Let Them Speak by Rebecca Coda and Rick Jetter

The Limitless School by Abe Hege and Adam Dovico

Live Your Excellence by Jimmy Casas

Next-Level Teaching by Jonathan Alsheimer

The Pepper Effect by Sean Gaillard

Principaled by Kate Barker, Kourtney Ferrua, and Rachael George

The Principled Principal by Jeffrey Zoul and Anthony McConnell

Relentless by Hamish Brewer

The Secret Solution by Todd Whitaker, Sam Miller, and Ryan Donlan

Start. Right. Now. by Todd Whitaker, Jeffrey Zoul, and Jimmy Casas

Stop. Right. Now. by Jimmy Casas and Jeffrey Zoul

Teachers Deserve It by Rae Hughart and Adam Welcome

Teach Your Class Off by CJ Reynolds

They Call Me "Mr. De" by Frank DeAngelis

Thrive through the Five by Jill M. Siler

Unmapped Potential by Julie Hasson and Missy Lennard

When Kids Lead by Todd Nesloney and Adam Dovico

Word Shift by Joy Kirr

Your School Rocks by Ryan McLane and Eric Lowe

Technology & Tools

50 Things to Go Further with Google Classroom by Alice Keeler and
Libbi Miller

50 Things You Can Do with Google Classroom by Alice Keeler and
Libbi Miller

140 Twitter Tips for Educators by Brad Currie, Billy Krakower, and
Scott Rocco

Block Breaker by Brian Aspinall

Building Blocks for Tiny Techies by Jamila "Mia" Leonard

Code Breaker by Brian Aspinall

The Complete EdTech Coach by Katherine Goyette and Adam Juarez

Control Alt Achieve by Eric Curts

The Esports Education Playbook by Chris Aviles, Steve Isaacs,
Christine Lion-Bailey, and Jesse Lubinsky

Google Apps for Littles by Christine Pinto and Alice Keeler

Master the Media by Julie Smith

Raising Digital Leaders by Jennifer Casa-Todd

Reality Bytes by Christine Lion-Bailey, Jesse Lubinsky, and
Micah Shippee, PhD

Sail the 7 Cs with Microsoft Education by Becky Keene and
Kathi Kersznowski

Shake Up Learning by Kasey Bell

Social LEADia by Jennifer Casa-Todd

Stepping Up to Google Classroom by Alice Keeler and
Kimberly Mattina

Teaching Math with Google Apps by Alice Keeler and
Diana Herrington

Teachingland by Amanda Fox and Mary Ellen Weeks

Teaching with Google Jamboard by Alice Keeler and Kimberly Mattina

Teaching Methods & Materials

All 4s and 5s by Andrew Sharos

Boredom Busters by Katie Powell

The Classroom Chef by John Stevens and Matt Vaudrey

The Collaborative Classroom by Trevor Muir

Copyrighteous by Diana Gill

CREATE by Bethany J. Petty

Ditch That Homework by Matt Miller and Alice Keeler

Ditch That Textbook by Matt Miller

Don't Ditch That Tech by Matt Miller, Nate Ridgway, and
 Angelia Ridgway

EDrenaline Rush by John Meehan

Educated by Design by Michael Cohen, The Tech Rabbi

The EduProtocol Field Guide by Marlena Hebern and Jon Corippo

The EduProtocol Field Guide: Book 2 by Marlena Hebern and
 Jon Corippo

The EduProtocol Field Guide: Math Edition by Lisa Nowakowski and
 Jeremiah Ruesch

Expedition Science by Becky Schnekser

Frustration Busters by Katie Powell

Fully Engaged by Michael Matera and John Meehan

Game On? Brain On! by Lindsay Portnoy, PhD

Guided Math AMPED by Reagan Tunstall

Innovating Play by Jessica LaBar-Twomy and Christine Pinto

Instant Relevance by Denis Sheeran

Keeping the Wonder by Jenna Copper, Ashley Bible, Abby Gross, and
 Staci Lamb

LAUNCH by John Spencer and A.J. Juliani

Make Learning MAGICAL by Tisha Richmond

Pass the Baton by Kathryn Finch and Theresa Hoover

Project-Based Learning Anywhere by Lori Elliott

Pure Genius by Don Wettrick

The Revolution by Darren Ellwein and Derek McCoy

Shift This! by Joy Kirr

Skyrocket Your Teacher Coaching by Michael Cary Sonbert

Spark Learning by Ramsey Musallam

Sparks in the Dark by Travis Crowder and Todd Nesloney

Table Talk Math by John Stevens

Unpack Your Impact by Naomi O'Brien and LaNesha Tabb

The Wild Card by Hope and Wade King

The Writing on the Classroom Wall by Steve Wyborney

You Are Poetry by Mike Johnston

Inspiration, Professional Growth & Personal Development

Be REAL by Tara Martin

Be the One for Kids by Ryan Sheehy

The Coach ADVenture by Amy Illingworth

Creatively Productive by Lisa Johnson

Educational Eye Exam by Alicia Ray

The EduNinja Mindset by Jennifer Burdis

Empower Our Girls by Lynmara Colón and Adam Welcome

Finding Lifelines by Andrew Grieve and Andrew Sharos

The Four O'Clock Faculty by Rich Czyz

How Much Water Do We Have? by Pete and Kris Nunweiler

P Is for Pirate by Dave and Shelley Burgess

A Passion for Kindness by Tamara Letter

The Path to Serendipity by Allyson Apsey

Rogue Leader by Rich Czyz

Sanctuaries by Dan Tricarico

Saving Sycamore by Molly B. Hudgens

The SECRET SAUCE by Rich Czyz

Shattering the Perfect Teacher Myth by Aaron Hogan

Stories from Webb by Todd Nesloney

Talk to Me by Kim Bearden

Teach Better by Chad Ostrowski, Tiffany Ott, Rae Hughart, and
    Jeff Gargas
Teach Me, Teacher by Jacob Chastain
Teach, Play, Learn! by Adam Peterson
The Teachers of Oz by Herbie Raad and Nathan Lang-Raad
TeamMakers by Laura Robb and Evan Robb
Through the Lens of Serendipity by Allyson Apsey
The Zen Teacher by Dan Tricarico

Children's Books

Beyond Us by Aaron Polansky
Cannonball In by Tara Martin
Dolphins in Trees by Aaron Polansky
I Can Achieve Anything by MoNique Waters
I Want to Be a Lot by Ashley Savage
The Princes of Serendip by Allyson Apsey
Ride with Emilio by Richard Nares
The Wild Card Kids by Hope and Wade King
Zom-Be a Design Thinker by Amanda Fox

CPSIA information can be obtained
at www.ICGtesting.com
Printed in the USA
LVHW010318170322
713569LV00016B/2217